# LIBERATION SPIRITUALITY

**BRITISH LIBERATION THEOLOGY**
Edited by Chris Rowland and John Vincent

1. LIBERATION THEOLOGY UK

2. GOSPEL FROM THE CITY

3. LIBERATION SPIRITUALITY

In Preparation

4. BIBLE AND PRACTICE

5. BLACK AND ASIAN THEOLOGY

Further volumes under consideration

British Liberation Theology is published under the auspices of the British Liberation Theology Project, the Institute for British Liberation Theology of the Urban Theology Unit and the Las Casas Network. The Management Group of the British Liberation Theology Project is: Rev Inderjit Bhogal, Dr Andrew Bradstock, Bishop Laurie Green, Prof. Christopher Rowland, Ms Bridget Rees, Mr Mike Simpson, Dr. John Vincent and Sister Margaret Walsh. Bridget Rees and John Vincent are Joint Co-ordinators of the Institute.

The annual volumes of British Liberation Theology are available on subscription or as single books. Single copies may be obtained price £7.50, p&p 50p. A subscription to all three of the first volumes (1,2 and 3) can be obtained price £20 inc. p&p. Normal discounts (35%) are available to booksellers. Quantities of 20 or over are available to other organisations at a special discount (25%). Cheques to URBAN THEOLOGY UNIT.

Address all enquiries to: Peter Colby, Administrator, URBAN THEOLOGY UNIT, 210 Abbeyfield Road, Sheffield, S4 7AZ.

BRITISH LIBERATION THEOLOGY 3

# LIBERATION SPIRITUALITY

Edited by
CHRIS ROWLAND
and
JOHN VINCENT

Sheffield
URBAN THEOLOGY UNIT

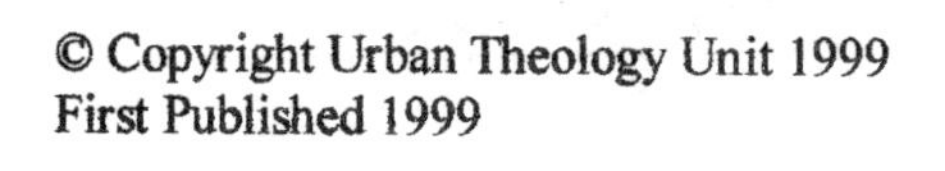

First Published 1999

ISBN: 0 907490 07 7

Urban Theology Unit is Registered Charity No. 505334



URBAN THEOLOGY UNIT
210 Abbeyfield Road
Sheffield
S4 7AZ

Typeset by Anne Lewis and Janet Colby at the Urban Theology Unit.

Printed by Tartan Press, Attercliffe, Sheffield

# CONTENTS

-8-
EDITORIAL NOTE

-10-
Bridget Rees
LIBERATION SPIRITUALITY

1. Approaching the Third Millennium
2. The Perspective of Liberation
3. Spirituality as Big Business

-17-
Christine Dodd
LIBERATING SPIRITUALITY AND
SPIRITUALITY FOR LIBERATION

1. Liberating Spirituality
    Immanent and Transcendent
    Contemplation and Radical Action
    Individual and Communal
2. Spirituality for Liberation
    Into God
    Into Ourselves
    Into Discipleship
    Into the World

-30-
Alan Powers
ANGELS, EAGLES, RESURRECTIONS

1. The Angel Taps
2. The Eagle Lands
3. The Dead God Resurrects
4. The Galilean Walks

-42-
Ian Fraser
A SPIRITUALITY OF RESISTANCE

1. The Call to Resist
2. A Spirituality of Resistance

-46-
Inderjit Bhogal
PRAYER, PROTEST AND POLITICS

1. Political Holiness
2. Holiness in Scripture
3. Separation or Connectedness?
4. Holiness as the Need of Church Today
5. Bert Bissell
6. Holiness in Prayer, Protest and Politics
7. Holiness Requires Politics
8. Politics Requires Holiness
9. Concluding Comments

-61-
Jan Royan
A SPIRITUALITY FOR
INNER CITY VOCATION

1. Don't Fence Me In!
2. Mutuality of Evangelism
3. We Cannot Do Everything
4. Perseverance
5. Knowing When To let Go
6. Vulnerable, but not a Victim
7. Loving Myself
8. Rooted and Connected
9. Sources, Wells and Places of Refreshment

-68-
Grace Vincent
WORSHIP AT GRIMESTHORPE

1. Sunday Morning: the Event
2. A "Fellowship Service" at Grimesthorpe
3. Grimesthorpe: the Context
4. Worship: the People's Work

-74-
Mike Simpson and Joan Sharples
CONSULTATION AND CELEBRATION

1. The Background
2. The First Consultation 1989
3. Las Casas
4. The Second Consultation 1991
5. The Third Consultation 1993
6. The Fourth Consultation 1995
7. The Fifth Consultation 1997

-95-
John Vincent
A NEW THEOLOGY AND SPIRITUALITY

1. God's Realm as Presence
2. God's Realm as Politics
3. Receiving God's Realm as a Child
4. Evangelisation by the Poor
5. Secular Jesus Spirituality
6. Secularity and enChristedness
7. "Spiritual Exercises"

-107-
Letters
Chronicle
Publications

# EDITORIAL NOTE

BRITISH LIBERATION THEOLOGY is the overall title for a series of Bi-annual Volumes, designed to bring together new writing in the UK, using the methods of Liberation Theology, and recording the practice and spirituality of people involved in liberation struggles in Britain.

LIBERATION THEOLOGY UK was the first volume, intended to set the scene for a British Liberation Theology within the wider context of world-wide liberation theologies, and to indicate some of the ways in which liberation theology has worked and is working in contemporary thinking and discipleship. The level of the chapters in the volume was intentionally academic and pastoral. It shows how British theologies of liberation both see themselves alongside those of other continents, and also pursue distinctive indigenous agendas.

The two following volumes begin at the other end – the levels specifically of pastoral and popular practice. The second volume, GOSPEL FROM THE CITY, contains the stories, the theology and the spirituality of several contemporary disciples and groups, who see themselves as putting into practice or being motivated by liberation theology. They are stories of the practice of liberation in the urban scene today.

This third volume, LIBERATION SPIRITUALITY, records some practice and reflection in terms of lifestyle, discipleship, and prayer which are found among liberation-style practitioners. Several contributors also reflect on the personal and corporate practice of Liberation Theology in Britain, and discern some significant elements and some emerging characteristics.

The fourth volume, BIBLE AND PRACTICE, will record stories of the practice of Liberation Theology activists who use the Bible in a variety of ways, and also articles on specific aspects of the Bible, by biblical scholars and pastoral workers.

The fifth volume we plan to be BLACK AND ASIAN THEOLOGY. In the main, as heretofore, the work of specific "branches" of liberation theologies goes on primarily elsewhere – Feminist Theology, Black Theology, Regional Theologies, Lesbian and Gay Theologies, Womanist Theology. We have no wish to presume to "take over" the whole scene, though we do hope to have chapters or possibly volumes which reflect these growing and productive areas in which liberation theology proceeds from the stand-point of particular groups. Indeed, it might be that our effort will encourage them also to wider publication. Of course, that would certainly not be the case for Feminist Theology, which has already created highly significant developments, and which has certainly blazed the trail both for a more general liberation theology, and also for liberation theologies from the stand-points of the women and men oppressed in other ways.

We hope at various times to include theological discussions concerning the wider theological debates on Britain, and the legitimacy or appropriateness of British liberation theologies, especially taking into account the use made of liberation theology perspectives in other contemporary British theologians. But there has been a tendency to discuss such matters in abstract fashion – witness the endless papers, articles and chapters on the theme "What is the relevance of liberation theology to British Christians/Churches/Theology?" It may be a useful change to postpone such theoretical questions for a few years, and let some of those who want to work this way get on and see what they can produce.

We would like to invite readers to offer contributions (3,000-6,000 words). Later volumes may cover biblical theology, political theology, and practical issues in personal, community, political and public life, from liberation theology viewpoints. Please address enquiries to either of us:

CHRIS ROWLAND
Queen's College, Oxford, OX1 4AW

JOHN VINCENT
Urban Theology Unit, Sheffield, S4 7AZ

June 1999

# Bridget Rees

# LIBERATION SPIRITUALITY

## 1. Approaching the Third Millennium

This book comes out as people throughout the world of various faiths and none are preparing for the beginning of a new millennium. For some this is an occasion for remembering the birth of Jesus who is seen by Christians as Saviour or Liberator and for many of these as for some Jews it is also a time which they wish to observe as a year of Jubilee as described in the book of Leviticus[1]. The year of Jubilee was probably only ever a dream rather than a reality, but dreams often and fortunately have had, and continue to have, a powerful influence on sustaining people, particularly when they are finding life is tough. So the Jubilee year of 2000 is becoming for many oppressed and marginalised people a peg on which to hang some of their hopes.

Many "new" theologies and spiritualities have emerged in this present millennium as in the previous one, though some of these may not have been in fact as new as has sometimes been claimed. In the last forty years of this millennium, as many aspects of life have appeared to move faster and faster, more and more new theologies and approaches to spirituality have also begun to appear. Many of these theologies have been described as Liberation Theologies, though there are still an amazing number of people including professional theologians who think Liberation Theology belongs only to

---

**Bridget Rees was a founder member of Women in Theology. After being an Anglican Education Advisor and Christian Aid area organiser, she in 1997 became Director of the Mirfield Centre. She is currently unemployed.**

Central and South America. Liberation Theology in fact includes under its umbrella Asian theology, African theology, Palestinian theology, as well as Central and South American theology, black theology, feminist theology, womanist theology, native American theology, Hispanic theology, and a host of other theologies which could be described as coming from the underside of history[2], and not just in the so called "third world".

This volume, like its predecessors, consists of contributions from a group of people from England, Scotland, Wales and Ireland, who have been inspired by some or even all the Liberation Theologies mentioned above, and by their experiences of either being marginalised because of race, gender, sexuality, class, age, physical or mental ability etc, or else of living and working among such people. The pieces in this book and its predecessor are written by practitioners. The importance of these contributions is, among other things, that they are written by people rooted in situations where injustice and oppression is clear. Yet these people live and work in countries which compared with situations in those normally thought of producing Liberation Theology, might seem comparatively just and wealthy. But the "third world" is to be found even in the "first world".

As with the best known Liberation Theologies, there is perhaps inevitably a tendency to generalise and to theorise from the particular experiences. But those of us who have visited for example places like Peru know that behind the academic and sometimes apparently heavy theology are real people practically working to make their bit of the world a more just, safe and nourishing experience and there are real attempts to grapple with evil, injustice, hatred and death, here and now.

## 2. The Perspective of Liberation

For many of the Liberation Theologies in print and developing, there are texts and stories which are regularly and often appealed to. Two of the most formative and most commonly appealed to are the story of the exodus from Egypt (though not for Palestinians!) and the story of Jesus' sermon at Nazareth which refers quite clearly to the idea of Jubilee.[3] Jesus reads from Isaiah:

> "The Spirit of the Lord is upon me because he has anointed me;
> he has sent me to announce good news to the poor, to proclaim
> release for prisoners and recovery of sight for the blind: to let

> the broken victims go free, to proclaim the year of the Lord's favour … 'Today' he said, 'in your hearing this text has come true'."

This latter text, together with the passage from Leviticus to which it refers, has been picked up by many in preparations for the third millennium, and particularly by the coalition of organisations which has formed the Jubilee 2000 Coalition which is campaigning for the cancellation of the backlog of unpayable debt owed by the world's poorest countries.

In a book of reflections on theology and debt called "Proclaim Liberty" which Christian Aid published as part of the debt campaign, Anne Pettifor, the Director of Jubilee 2000, describes how the campaign started – "as the vision of one of the descendants of a British anti-slavery campaigner, Martin Dent."[4] The campaign has been seen by many of the agencies involved as a natural successor to the Churches' involvement in the anti-slavery campaign, as debt burdens are creating a new form of slavery. This is picked up strongly by the Archbishop of Cantebury in his introduction to the same book.

> "If we look at the Old Testament, we see that experiences of slavery and liberation from the promised land, deeply marked the religious consciousness of the people of Israel … The Churches have a particular responsibility to campaign in an informed manner for economic and political strategies which reinforce the Christian message of human dignity for all, since we are made in the image of God. The modern enslavement of debt and the Christian message that Jesus Christ has come to offer life in all its fullness (John 10: 10) stand in the starkest contradiction."[5]

The earlier anti-slavery campaigns and other similar social justice activities were to a considerable extent based on theological arguments, as are the present campaigns. The sort of theology underpinning both the older and current campaigns is Liberation Theology, though that description of the type of theology used is a comparatively new one, and many of the Jubilee 2000 supporters would not necessarily be aware of it, either here or further afield.

One of the pieces of material produced by Christian Aid as its contribution to the Jubilee 2000 coalition is a prayer card which on the front has the words

"Your will be done ...
Break the chains of debt.
The absence of debt is a sign that God's Kingdom has come."

The prayer on the card by Janet Morley reads

"O God, to whom we owe more than we can count,
in our desire to control all that will come to be,
we hold your children in the grip of debt which they cannot repay,
and make them suffer now the poverty we dread.
Do not hold us to our debts, but unchain our fear,
that we may release others into an open future of unbounded hope
through Jesus Christ our Saviour.
Amen."

In literature such as this, a clear connection is being made between theology, spirituality and campaigning activity, As I write this, in April 1999, I would suggest that the largest numbers of people in this country who are involved in liberation theology and spirituality are doing it, often unselfconsciously, in their campaigning activities on debt or trade issues. Their campaigning activity is nourished and inspired by their spirituality, as well as by their reflection on Scripture and their faith. Worship material produced by organisations like Christian Aid and CAFOD as well as by Communities like the Iona Community have been and are enormously important as food on the journey towards the promised land.

However, this book has been written by people several of whom though active in the Jubilee 2000 campaign are concerned more with the marginalised and issues of injustice here in this country. These people, like some of those involved in the Jubilee coalition, are often inspired by the theology and worship worked out by Christians in very different situations in shanty towns and townships around the world, and are using similar approaches in their very different circumstances here.

What all these people are doing, and concerned to witness to in a variety of ways, is their belief that God is on the side of the poor, the marginalised, the oppressed wherever they are, and that God wants us to work for justice for all people, creatures and the creation. Many of those who have continued to be Churchgoers have found that the worship and concerns of many of the mainstream churches have become increasingly sterile for them. So, in addition to their traditional worship, they have turned to other sources for nourishment and worship which seem to them to be more related to their beliefs and theological convictions.

### 3. Spirituality as Big Business

It is interesting that those of us who have been laying on courses and conferences during these last few years in the Churches have found that many Churchgoers are reluctant to attend events which have a justice focus, but are very keen to attend anything that has the word "spirituality" in its title.

The separation between spirituality and politics assumed by many Churchgoers is to some of us very alarming. Politics is of course usually seen as anything which challenges rather than supports the status quo. Two posters come to mind – one from Christian Aid with a picture and quote from Desmond Tutu:

> "I wonder what Bible people are reading when they say religion and politics don't mix";

and one from CAFOD with a picture and quote from Dom Helder Camara:

> "When I feed the poor they call me a saint, but when I ask why the poor are hungry they call me a communist".

Spirituality seems to be a big business at the moment. The enormous popularity of Myers Briggs events[6] and Ignatian or other individually guided retreats, which though not in themselves necessarily introspective often seem to end up being so, is interesting. I find it particularly interesting as someone who was much involved in some of the human relations training which the Churches laid on in the 70s which had much more of a focus on working in groups than on individual growth, and much of which grew out of the struggle against apartheid in South Africa. This sort of approach was never as popular.

Tissa Balasuriya in his book *Eucharist and Human Liberation*[7], which has long been an inspiration to me, talks about the way in which the Eucharist, which should be an act of liberation, has in fact become one of domestication. He observes that it is nonsense that the oppressed and the oppressor who kneel together and receive communion together leave as if their relationship had not been changed. It seems to me that much of the Spirituality on offer and popular at the moment is more concerned with domestication than liberation, with the status quo than new birth.

I have in the last two years been working and worshipping with an Anglican religious order of men and a theological college which is almost entirely male. Worshipping with these men usually twice a day, five days a week, and generally being the only woman present, has been an interesting experience. In the beginning, it was nourishing and rather comforting to return to my Anglo Catholic roots. It was a bit like a warm bath, and I was amused to hear a sermon there which spoke of Baptism as being a bit like a warm bath, six months after I had preached about how terrifying it was to be called to be immersed in the baptismal waters, dying and rising with Christ in Baptism.

As we said the psalms together in a four week cycle, day by day, week by week, month by month, I increasingly wondered what was happening to us as we said them together; who we were identifying with – the victim who was being persecuted and mistreated, or the one who was wicked and treating the victim so badly – the powerful or the powerless, the chosen or the rejected. Increasingly I found myself very uncomfortable in what felt like a process of domestication rather than one of liberation.

This was a process which I became more and more aware of when I worshipped with others who were very clearly struggling with Gospel issues of justice in situations in West Yorkshire as well as further afield, and in working with others promoting the Jubilee 2000 campaign.

This book, like its predecessors, is evidence of just some, and there are many more, ordinary people, well known and less well known, who are struggling, with their theology and their spirituality, to live out the Gospel today by tackling local and global injustices which face people every day of their lives. Like those who are involved in the Jubilee 2000 campaign and other struggles for justice, whether they be focused on race, class, gender, sexuality, physical or mental ability and many more, we are attempting to live out the Gospel in the world. We witness to the fact that we believe all of us are made in God's image, that God intends that all of us, not just some of us, should have abundant life, that it is possible to make the world a better place for all, that all injustice and evil has to be eliminated.

As Desmond Tutu put it in a prayer written in the struggle against apartheid

> Goodness is stronger than evil
> Love is stronger than hate
> Light is stronger than darkness
> Life is stronger than death

Victory is ours through him who loved us. Amen.

This is what we witness to and work for as we move into a new millennium.

What we do is not new and is in a long tradition going back not just through the last two millennia but back to the Leviticus dream of Jubilee and even earlier.

Maranatha.

---

[1] Leviticus 25: 8-17

[2] Professor James Cone of Union Theological Seminary, New York, teaches a class which he calls Theology from the Underside of History, in which he focuses on the work of the Ecumenical Association of Third World Theologians (EATWOT)

[3] Luke 4: 14-30

[4] **Proclaim Liberty. Reflections on Theology and Debt**. Ed Susan Hawler. Christian Aid, 1998, p. 88.

[5] Ibid pp. 7 and 9

[6] Ken Leech, **The Sky is Red**, Darton Longman and Todd 1997, pp. 17-18

[7] Tissa Balasuriya, **Eucharist and Human Liberation**, SCM 1974

Christine Dodd

# LIBERATING SPIRITUALITY AND SPIRITUALITY OF LIBERATION

What is Spirituality? Take a look around any decently sized bookshop and it will not take very long to discover the section where all the books on spirituality are displayed. It is usually situated near astrology and religion. But the variety of books on these shelves illustrates the wide range of meanings attached to this word – and therein lies a difficulty. Books on geography, cookery, history or travel are easy to catalogue and classify, but books on spirituality cover everything from classical books on mysticism and Christian prayer to New Age theories on God as an extraterrestrial. Part of the shop manager's difficulty in placing these books lies in trying to define the word 'spirituality'. Both it and liberation are what I call 'slippery' words. They tend to mean different things to the people using them, and they both

---

**Dr Christine Dodd is Adult Education Adviser for the RC Diocese of Hallam. Her books include Making Scripture Work, and Called to Mission. She is a DMin graduate of UTU/New York Theological Seminary, and a co-ordinator in the UTU/Sheffield University MMin/DMin programme.**

beg enormous questions – not least of which is how they relate to each other.

Let's begin with Spirituality. The questions about this are concerned with what it is for. Is it about seeking 'the Other' in our world of the here and now or beyond it? Is it about the discovering the God within or the God without? Is it about unifying ourselves with the earth or rising above it? Self-fulfilment or self-negation? Turning to liberation, the questions are likewise concerned with basic issues. What are we being liberated for? What sort of new life will freedom bring? Is it ever really possible to be liberated or do we move from one form of slavery to another? What responsibilities does freedom bring? What is the relationship between spirituality and liberation?

It seems to me that the relationship between spirituality and liberation is twofold. On the one hand we need to ask what sort of spirituality is required in the struggle for liberation, and on the other hand, we need to ask how spirituality itself can be liberated. There is no doubt that spirituality has been enslaved in many ways over the centuries. In reality, a spirituality for liberation and liberating spirituality are two sides of one coin, and we need to explore both.

But before we can get down to the relationship between these two words we have to make a stab at defining what we mean by 'spirituality'. We need to try and be clear what we are talking about. It needs to be said here that this article is referring specifically to Christian spirituality (though those of other faiths might well see something of their own situation within what is said). Few words are as misunderstood as this one. In his excellent book, *Seeking Spirituality, Guidelines for a Christian Spirituality for the Twenty-first Century*, Ronald Rolheiser writes about how for most people, including many Christians, this word conjures up images of something mystical, pious, other worldly, something on the fringes, not something vital lying at the centre of things.

> This is a tragic misunderstanding. Spirituality is not something on the fringes ... everyone does have one, either life-giving or destructive. We do not wake up one morning in this world calm and serene, having the luxury of choosing to act or not to act. We wake up crying, on fire with desire, with madness. What we do with this madness is our spirituality ... Long before we do anything explicitly religious at all we have to do something with the fire that burns within us. How we channel it is our spirituality.[1]

In Rolheiser's view, we all have a spirituality whether we want one or not. It is what we do with our deepest longings and desires, with the energy deep within us, which matters.

This definition may seem too broad and not 'religious' enough for many people, but if what burns within us is God-given energy which we have the freedom to either develop 'in a Godward direction' or deny. This surely is the basis on which we build the best practices of Christian spirituality. It also releases us from a good many unhelpful preconceptions and allows us to make connections which will overcome the polarities by which spirituality is too often beset and to which we now turn. Above all, it will place spirituality at the centre of our action within the struggle for liberation, for ourselves and others.

## 1. Liberating Spirituality

It is my belief that there are three specific areas from which spirituality needs to be freed if it is to be of service to the struggle for liberation and play its essential (and I would say central) and full part in that struggle. All three of these areas have to do with false polarities with which so much spirituality seems to be infected. First, there is the false polarity between the immanent and transcendent. Second, that between contemplation and radical action; and thirdly, the polarity between individualism and community.

### Immanent and Transcendent

One of the difficulties we face in liberating our spirituality in order to find a spirituality which will liberate us is the polarity which exists in so much writing and talking, namely that between the immanent and the transcendent. Much spirituality has exhorted us to leave ourselves behind, to negate – or transcend – ourselves. It is, of course, true that 'lifting heart and mind' to the recognition of the Creator, of the otherness of God, is an essential element of all spirituality, but this need not be done at the expense of our true selves. What is required is the discovery of the transcendent in our midst. This is not only the way to overcome the polarity which threatens to cripple our spirituality, but it also links spirituality to liberation.

It is here that we must mention a theme which will run through our consideration of each of our three polarities, namely that of incarnation.

Incarnational theology (and spirituality) lies at the heart of liberating action. It is a belief that the Word is made flesh in the here and now, and that God can be discovered in the world and in the life we live both as individuals and in community. It is therefore about co-operating with God in the work of liberation which is God's work. Incarnational theology then sees no polarity between the transcendent and the immanent. Rather, the transcendent can be discerned and experienced within the immanent.

With this as a basis, our times of withdrawal or reflection can be seen not as negation of the world, but rather as times that will enable us to see God's action more clearly – times which help us hear what God is calling us both to do and become. In this way, the Other is to be found in our midst, and our spirituality becomes the basis for continuing God's liberating work. Not only this, but, at the same time, we find ourselves liberated from a spirituality which confines itself to the religious or 'churchy' sphere. It is spirituality which begins to transform us. The Word becomes flesh in us not only for our own sake but for the sake of those whose lives we touch.

Contemplation and Radical Action

This incarnational view of spirituality also helps us overcome our second polarity; the polarity between contemplation and radical action. To discover God at work in the here and now means that the two are joined. We need those moments of contemplation if we are to hear the voice of God and not indulge in mere ideology. At the same time contemplation must issue in radical discipleship which works to continue God's liberating action.

Evelyn Underhill, that great spiritual writer who insisted on keeping the balance between contemplation and action, viewed spirituality as something intensely social. Writing about her, Annie Callahan observes,

> "The implication of this attitude includes an acceptance of interconnectedness of politics and spirituality ... for her (Evelyn Underhill), the important task is to maintain the ongoing correlation between the inner and the outer"[2]

Contemplation gives us the 'squint' with which we glimpse those Kingdom moments and events where God is already acting, and to begin to co-operate with God in that action. The action may well involve the sort of self giving and courage which the great spiritual writers often mention. It involves a giving away of ourselves, a cost, a radical following which is all part of discipleship.

What is interesting about this self giving which is the result of our spirituality is that far from negating ourselves, it makes us more ourselves. This is one of the paradoxes of Christian spirituality, the more we give the more we are truly ourselves.

> "St John of the Cross is normally associated with an almost inhumanely negative and comfortless view of the spiritual life; and it is true that he sets out the human cost of faith with more pitiless candour than almost any other comparable writer (even Luther). Yet it is a movement towards fulfilment, not emptiness, towards beauty and life, not annihilation ... it is the liberation of desire itself from external objects and worldly gods".[3]

Individual and Communal

Our third polarity is about the relationship between the individual and the community. Individualism is a mark of our present world and spirituality is, of course, to do with our personal response to that energy and force that drives us. But this is only part of my story. A spirituality which liberates us is not something I explore on my own, for the simple reason that I am a social being. I do not live without reference to others. Jesus calls not just individuals but individuals into community. How we relate to each other is part of how we relate to God. Not only this, but God often speaks to us through others.

Our age tends to divorce spirituality from ecclesiology, but it is within the matrix of the faith community that faith becomes real, tested and tried rather than in private fantasy.

> "Spirituality is ultimately communitarian even within those faiths such as Buddism, Hinduism, Islam and Taoism that are not ecclesial in their essential make-up as are Christianity and Judaism. Why? Because the search for God is not a private search ... it is about a communal search for the face of God and one searches communally only within a historical community."[4]

This aspect of community liberates spirituality and enables spirituality to be earthed. Wherever spirituality is largely purely individual it is in danger, at worst of living in a private fantasy land, at best of being concerned only with myself. However high my motives, this will not test and try me, as much as having spirituality formed within the context of the web of relationships which will challenge and affirm me. In other words God speaks to me through other people. This communal side to our spirituality allows us to engage in the 'liberation project' which God has for all. We can do things together which we can never do alone, and we respond to God together when we hear God's Word together. In the Scriptures, God calls individuals but their calling is within the community. Even in our churches we see this tendency to create a dichotomy between individual spirituality and the communal. People still talk about going to church in order to be private or not wanting to be disturbed in their personal prayer. Perhaps this is a reflection of the image of God we have. Or perhaps it is the result of our heightened awareness of individualism in society at large. Maybe it is a bit of both.

Unifying

Overcoming these three polarities is therefore a matter of unifying spirituality, bringing together immanent and transcendent, contemplation and action, individual and community. Far from this leading to a watering down of the different aspects of spirituality, it allows them to flower and to feed each other. Our spirituality should force us into that life which both brings things together and rejoices in diversity. This unified understanding may well liberate spirituality to be what it really is, a channelling of God-given energy. It will liberate us – but into what?

## 2. Spirituality for Liberation

Having looked briefly at liberating spirituality, let us now look at what a relevant spirituality for liberation might mean. If, as I believe, spirituality lies at the heart of the liberation struggle, to where should a spirituality freed from polarities bring us? What will it free us into?

Into God

First, it should liberate us into the very life of God, who is the God of freedom. In classical Christian theology this life is Trinitarian. The doctrine of the Trinity is undergoing something of a revival at present. In the context of this discussion, it is about being released into the essence of Trinitarian belief, namely unity in diversity. Our spirituality should free us into that life which both brings us together and rejoices in diversity. In practice this means two things. On the one hand, the channelling of our God-given desire or energy should make us whole, more complete, more unified as persons and as communities. On the other hand, it should enable us to see that there are many facets within ourselves which give our uniqueness, and many different gifts within our communities. There is a reflection of the very life of God, where there is both unity and diversity. Spirituality is a journey which leads us into the freedom of both – a rejoicing in our diversity (both that of communities and that of diversity which exists within me as a person), and a rejoicing in our oneness. A spirituality which frees us into the life of God therefore encourages both our individuality and our solidarity with others.

But the Trinitarian doctrine is not only about unity in diversity. It is also about 'give and take'. This, in classical terms, is described as the community of love within the Trinity acts as a model for our own experience. Our own flow of the giving away of ourselves in love and receiving in love mirrors the life and love which flow within God. It is this give and take which leads us into true freedom. It is no accident that Jesus speaks about the person who is willing to give herself or himself away who will truly receive or find themselves. This is not the self negation which is so often associated with spirituality. It is a recognition that in some mysterious way when we give of ourselves what we receive in return is our own freedom. Lest this all sound rather heavily theological, let me put it in another way.

Gerard Manley Hopkins talks in his poem about the world being "charged with the grandeur of God".[5] It is easy to see and say this in the midst of watching a glorious sunset or a spectacular view or listening to a piece of music. But where is the "grandeur of God" in the inner city or the poor of the shanty town or the violence of the abused child or the loneliness of bereavement? The grandeur of God lies, I suggest, in the people who 'incarnate' God in those situations. God takes carnis, (flesh), in those people who exercise the life and love, the give and take of Trinitarian life in those situations – those who give themselves away in myriads of diverse ways, those who unite others in their brokenness, who exercise their variety of gifts in the pain. And in exercising this give and take, this diversity in unity, they also discover not only that they are liberating people, but also that they themselves are being liberated into the life of God who is there with and in them. A new exodus is under way for individuals, for communities, for those who are still enslaved. So a relevant and holistic spirituality, a freed spirituality, leads us into the very life and love of God. But this is not all.

## Into Ourselves

Secondly, our spirituality should liberate into ourselves. It should set us free within ourselves – and most of us are only too aware that we are enslaved by many things. Here the principles of unity and diversity and of give and take also apply. A freed spirituality should enable us to be more complete, more whole, yet, at the same time, more aware of the 'diversity' that lies within each one of us and of the richness and wonder of that diversity. This quest is really about trying to discern and work with what C Day Lewis calls those "scorching ordeals that fire one's irresolute clay".[6] In other words, it is about making sense of ourselves, our diversity and uniqueness.

A liberated spirituality will also be one which is willing both to receive into ourselves whatever God shows us, and to give from our inner self. As we have seen, one of the paradoxes of this is that in giving ourselves away we find our true selves. In practice this means a willingness to be open to that prompting, (through whatever source, Scripture, liturgy, people, events), to look within – not in a negative or escapist way – but in order to become more complete, whole and freed persons. Karl Rahner called this "self awareness of selfless love".[7] Prayer invites us to surrender to God's own selfless love in order to become who we really are. If this is to happen to us, if we are to come into ourselves, we need two things. We need to immerse ourselves in God who is the source of our wholeness, and we need to be honest with ourselves about all that enslaves us or prevents us in that relationship with God. This really reflects two longings within the world at large – the desire to be free, (complete, whole, having got it all together), and the desire to be rid of that which dis-eases us, that which ties and binds people.

What is said of individuals can also be said of communities. These too are called to come into themselves. Such communities will be marked out by both their contact with a living God and the reproach which their life-style will give to all that enslaves people.

This sounds very grand, but in fact is to do with little things. It is to do with a community having a strong basis in God and developing ways to live out what they already know that means. So, a tiny Christian congregation set amid the urban sprawl of a city comes into itself, discovers its roots and basis, and because it has done so finds itself being seen as 'different' from the society around it. It stands both as a beacon of hope and as a challenge to the society in which it exists.

Into Discipleship

This leads us to our third consideration. A liberated spirituality should lead us into discipleship.

A spirituality for liberation is one which takes seriously two things, the power of paradox and the power of vulnerability. Jesus' 'manifesto', his mission statement for those who follow him, is to be found in that set of paradoxical statements, the beatitudes, (Matt 5: 1ff). Here weakness becomes strength, working for peace and justice is undertaken through powerlessness not exercise of might. Jesus turns on its head the norm by which society so often operates. Disciples are called to live out of this gospel paradox. This is not easy in a culture which praises success, power and possessions. Indeed, it can only truly be attempted by those who are fed by a spirituality which, as we have seen, is itself a paradox of giving in order to receive. This makes spirituality central to the liberation struggle. It works within the same matrix. It is of the same weft and woof as the struggle of which the beatitudes liberation theology speaks. Any spirituality which does not lead into this paradox and into action cannot be true to the gospel. Even those religious orders in the Roman Catholic Church, which are usually described as 'enclosed' and which are often accused of failing to engage in the liberation struggle, know the reality of paradox only too well. Their charism is of the same strain, the living out of the beatitudes within their own communities and providing a model and 'powerhouse' to enable others to do the same in their own contexts.

At the heart of this paradox is the theme of vulnerability. To talk about the power of vulnerability sounds like a contradiction in terms. Vulnerability is not a popular word or concept, but it is central to the gospel picture. Jesus is vulnerable. He is willing to be at the mercy of the world around him. Yet, and here is the important point, his very vulnerability is a work which creates unity (at-one-ment). This should suggest to us that there is no liberation unless there is an entering into the brokenness not only of the lives and situations of the oppressed, but of God and ourselves. The importance of this for a spirituality of liberation is twofold. First, such a spirituality is one of unification. We can only be open to God by making ourselves vulnerable; and God takes the risk of becoming vulnerable within us. There is thus a unity of vulnerability – God vulnerable to us, and us vulnerable to God. This powerlessness also unites us to those who are themselves oppressed and vulnerable to any form of enslavement. So there is a 'Trinity' here; us, God and others.

The unity of vulnerability goes even wider. It also includes the vulnerability of creation itself. We all know just how fragile our environment is and the stresses which are being placed on our delicate eco-system. A spirituality which unites our own vulnerability, that of God, and that of communities and of creation is not a new idea. St Irenaeus made an ambitious attempt at creating a theology which united not only creation and incarnation, but also consummation and the interdependence of all things. So it has a rich Christian history behind it. But our present-day awareness of the fragility of ourselves and our world has brought forth new ideas and put new emphasis on the place of spirituality in the struggle to liberate creation itself. Rosemary Radford Ruether in *Gaia and God* explores this:-

> "An ecological spirituality needs to be on built three premises, the transience of ourselves, the living inter-dependency of all things and the value of the person in communion. Many spiritual traditions have emphasised the need to let go of the ego, but in ways which diminished the value of the person, particularly those, like women, who scarcely have been allowed individual personhood at all. We need to let go of the ego in a different sense."[8]

The vulnerability required to let go of the ego in a new way is another of the paradoxes in which spirituality lives and breathes. To do this positively leads, as we have seen, to a greater individualisation and sense of self, not less. But this is not just individualism. We are not 'outside' anything. We find ourselves as ourselves <u>within</u> community and <u>within</u> creation.

The willingness to cultivate a spirit of vulnerability has another dimension. It enables us to become a "sign of contradiction". It helps us to develop a life-style which challenges the oppressive structures. This must be the outworking of our spirituality, which stands over and against the powers and systems which enslave people.

<u>Into the World</u>

Finally, a liberated spirituality must free us not <u>from</u> our humanity but <u>into</u> it. It is not an escape from but an insertion into the world in which we live. There are two practical results of experience of insertion. The first is that we see the world with all its oppression with open eyes. This in itself can be a liberating experience – it can also be a very challenging one as we are confronted with the brokenness of our creation and society's. To have open eyes is of course not enough. Open eyes lead on to open hands. Creating justice is a non-negotiable element within the spiritual life. It is an integral part of relating to God because, in an incarnational approach, how we treat the poor is how we treat God. The gospels are clear about this. As Cardinal Sin once said: "Love without justice is baloney!" If, as has been explored,

Christian spirituality is about how we channel our energy and desire Godward, it follows that it is about channelling our energy towards working for justice, because that is where God is.

> "The ultimate motivation in working for justice may never be simple ideology, irrespective of how noble that particular ideology may appear. Rather both the truth that inspires the quest for justice and the energy that fuels it must ground themselves in something beyond any ideology."[9]

Immersion into the world means immersion into specific cultures. Culture here means the way a particular society or group sees itself, its values and its actions – the way it does things. Spirituality is not immune from cultural influences, as can be clearly seen from the different forms and practices from the past. The sort of asceticism and spiritual practices around at the time, of say Teresa of Avila and John of the Cross, were influenced by the culture of the time. This not to say that the whole spirituality is culturally conditioned; some things are timeless and truth is eternal, but the way in which the truth is expressed does change. This means that we need to take culture seriously for two reasons – and both are of equal weight.

The first is that a liberated spirituality is one which recognises and responds to the culture in which it is practised. Many people have known the disaster which ensues from trying to live out a monastic style of spirituality, (eg set morning and evening quiet times), in the midst of a culture totally unsuited to this form of prayer. There is nothing wrong in this style – if it works for the individual – but for many it fails to operate because our life styles do not allow it. Our spirituality and our culture are 'mis-matched'. Too many people suffer from too much guilt as a result of this. We need to be liberated into new ways.

In today's society that will mean a far more flexible approach to spirituality than might have been the case in the past. Our culture is more fluid, we are used to more options, to trying things out and to making choices for ourselves. This is bound to affect our attitudes to the way our spirituality develops. Once we accept this as a possibility we shall be liberated to try out new forms, to reject what does not work for us, to build on "what speaks to us", and not to be afraid to try out new methods. There is not really anything new in this, for great spiritual writers of the past have long talked about the spiritual journey and pilgrimage, an image which is itself one of movement and discovery.

The second reason we need to take culture seriously is that if spirituality is not only to be liberated but to liberate, it must be linked to culture(s). As the basis of our work for justice, spirituality does not happen in a vacuum, or is set over and against our action. As we have seen, it is integral to it. So, a spirituality which is the focus of the life of the Base Christian Community in South America will not exactly be the same as the spirituality which focuses the life of a Christian community in suburban north London. There may be, (there should be), common points and truths but the expression will be different because the cultures are different. The wrong expression of spirituality in the wrong culture simply does not work and fails to enable us to be that liberating outpost which we are called to become.

Conclusion

Henri Nouwen wrote in his book "*Clowning in Rome*",

> "To pray, I think, does not mean to think about God in contrast to thinking about other things, or to spend time with God instead of spending time with other people. Rather it means to think and live in the presence of God. All our actions must have their origin in prayer. Praying is not an isolated activity; it takes place in the midst of all the things and affairs that keep us active. In prayer a 'self-centred monologue' becomes a 'God-centred dialogue'".[10]

This God-centred dialogue involves not just us as individuals, but as individuals in community. It is this dialogue which is at the root of our work for liberation. That dialogue contains an imperative. It is not to succeed. It is to be faithful. A liberated spirituality should enable us to see things in a more unified way; to see the inter-relatedness of God immanent and transcendent, the unity of action and reflection, individual prayer and community spirituality. We are called to see and respond to that vision in which "all shall be well, and all shall be well and all manner of things shall be well"[11], but to do so requires that we discover a spirituality which enables us to find the Christ who "continues to roll back the stone from the caves we entomb him in".[12]

---

[1] Ronald Rolheiser, **Seeking Spirituality: Guidelines for a Christian Spirituality for the Twenty-First Century**, (London, Hodder and Stoughton, 1998), p. 6

[2] Annie Callahan RSCJ, **Spiritual Guides for Today**, (London, Darton, Longman and Todd, 1992) p. 34

[3] Rowan Williams, **The Wound of Knowledge**, (London, Darton, Longman and Todd, 1979) p. 167-8

[4] Ronald Rolheiser, **Seeking Spirituality**, p. 66

[5] Gerard Manley Hopkins, "God's Grandeur" from **The Poems and Prose of Gerard Manley Hopkins**, (London, Penguin 1079), p. 27

[6] C Day Lewis, "Walking Away" from **The Complete Poems**, (London, Sinclair Stevenson 1992), p. 49

[7] K Rahner SJ, **The Religious Life Today**, (New York, Seabury, Crossroad 1976), p. 49

[8] Rosemary Radford Ruether, **Gaia and God**: An Ecofeminist Theology of Earth Healing,(London, SCM Press 1993), p. 251

[9] Ronald Rolheiser, **Seeking Spirituality**, p. 164

[10] Henri Nouwen, **Clowning in Rome: Reflections on Solitude, Celibacy, Prayer and Contemplation**, (New York, Doubleday 1979), p. 70-71

[11] Julian of Norwich, **Enfolded in Love**, (London, Darton, Longman and Todd, 1980) , p. 13

[12] John Shea, **The Challenge of Jesus**, (Chicago, Thomas More 1976), p. 11

# Alan Powers

# ANGELS, EAGLES, RESURRECTIONS

**1. Now you see it, Now you don't!**

At first, you think you are playing a game of peek-a-boo with some youngster somewhere. But you're not; you are playing with the God of the Jewish and Christian Scriptures. Martin Luther, that rude reformer of the 16th century, was always emphasising it, and from time to time since, other Christians have caught the habit. Being at one time a monk, his title for the game was usually in the Latin language, and the term became a classic amongst those who have seen the winning trick. For most of us, however the ground floor reality which gave rise to the brain-teaser, the sense of being abandoned to humanbeing, is too close to home to be dressed up in foreign language.

As a Church Minister, I have struggled with the game for years, and it is nowhere more real than in the life of prayer. During one period of my ministry, I left out Intercessory Prayer altogether from worship services which I conducted, and if any of my then-congregation is reading this I hope they will forgive my arrogance. At that time I could not see how the God I worshipped would ever change things because I and a few others prayed for them. Because my God was a God of love, I found it amazing that any human being could attempt to control God that way. The years have hardly changed things in that regard, but I am now a lot more tolerant of other people's opinions than I was then. Plus, of course, that I have seen the point of what

---

**Alan Powers is a Methodist Minister in Stockton. He became a UTU/NYTS DMin graduate when in Meanwood, Leeds, and is currently a UTU MMin part-time Tutor.**

Luther emphatically said was the simultaneous action of Deus Revelatus and Deus Absconditus. The God who reveals Himself is the God who hides. Now you see Him: now you don't. Ask the sufferer.

So how do you pray in these human conditions? How do you make intercession for others? How do you pray for yourself? I have tried the many and various ways offered by recent prayer and spirituality manuals. Recently, I used *Gospel from the City*. I read three passages and asked people to meditate in between. They are included in this article. I can't say I have solved the problem of prayer, but I am grateful that I still wrestle with it.

I am grateful to the Reformers' constant reminder, though, that we cannot control this God and Father of Jesus, and grateful that I don't have to believe that God places His blessing on everything which goes under that heading. In other words, to all intents and purposes, God ain't everywhere. For me there is something very meaningful about the few worshipping with a very amateur pianist and stumbling preacher in a little chapel, but I can't say I find these occasions terribly meaningful these days. On the contrary, I think there is something softly pornographic in some of the 'Songs of Praise' services I have experienced, and I have never lit a candle in the belief that the God who had done nothing previously about the subject of my prayers, should now grant my request because I had shown some interest.

We like to think we have got God taped. It is the besetting sin of religious people. Like scientists who have discovered the power of steam through watching a kettle boil, and who have the know-how to reproduce the phenomenon again and again, so religious people, or, at least the professionally religious people, are tempted to tell people where they can find the living God. The trouble is, however, that when they press the button that worked before, it does not work every time. "Truly Thou art a God who hidest Thyself", says the unfortunate Job. Too true. The trouble with prayer books is precisely this: those who have produced them too easily lead others to assume that God listens to that prayer. The prayer and spirituality book writers are the experts who know how to get through to the Deity, who know the channels through which our prayers will easily move. Some of those who have struggled with prayer will deny this. The Christians who have struggled with prayer will be the first to admit that we cannot be certain that God is on the other side of our beseeching. They know. But too often the unaware worshippers, and the professionals who write the prayers for them, do not. They assume that these prayer-makers, like any other scientists, have experimented and come up with the goods. For "goods" read "gods". The experts know the way to the Almighty, or so the worshippers too often think.

## 2. The Angel Taps

Then suddenly, without warning, an angel taps us on the shoulder, like the one who tapped Jan Royan on the shoulder.

> Armed with pick and shovel and getting wetter and colder by the minute, we attacked the rockhard clay with our implements and managed eventually to dig a shallow hole. I fetched a towel and plastic bag and we put Topsy into it and buried her. By this time, I was crying. Topsy had been part of my life too in the Lake District and I could imagine how the family would feel when they returned home and heard how she had died. Jenny put her arms around me and said, "Don't cry, Jan. Topsy's happy now". Then to prevent dogs from digging up Topsy's body, we lugged heavy stones to lay over the grave.
>
> When I thought we had got enough, I turned to Jenny and said, "That'll do. Let's go in and get warm and have a cup of tea". It was Jenny who said very hesitantly, "Shouldn't we say a prayer for Topsy, Jan?" And that made me cry again at the thought of this girl, who had rarely set foot in the church, who had been taken into care, known what it was like to bear the brunt of violence done to herself, her sisters and her mother, teaching me about the love of God for all creation." (p.44)

In our patronising way, it would be easy to say that Jenny had been influenced by "folk-religion", or that Jan had felt unnecessarily guilty because her natural approach to the situation did not feel the need for prayer. Would it not be more true, as well as more helpful, to say that the Living God, who acts in freedom, had tapped Jan on the shoulder through the words of this little girl? Martin Luther's Lord was up to His peek-a-boo tricks again.

Is not the essence of Judaism and Christianity that the Creator of this world is the Sovereign Lord who, while "exempt from external control" (I have just glanced at the Oxford Dictionary for help with the word "Sovereign") chooses to be on the side of humanity? We cannot control Him, but He is by our side as Friend. God chose to reveal himself in a dream to Joseph. However hard we try, though, we cannot guarantee a word from the Lord in a dream. He did reveal Himself in a burning bush to Moses, didn't he? But we could sit by a bush for hours in search of a revelation – and receive nothing.

And as if to emphasise His total sovereignty, He revealed Himself to Job in a storm, but refused to do the same for Elijah. Instead, the latter had to be content with a sound of gentle stillness. Woe betide the person who reckons on life without Him, but woe betide the one who tries to control Him. The first is the atheist; the second is the religious_enthusiast. Both are dangerous though the latter, it would appear from the Gospel story, is a little more so than the former. Better to deny God altogether than think we have Him taped.

Of the danger of religious professionals there are not a few examples in the Jewish and Christian scriptures. Let us take just two examples. The first is from Jeremiah's time, when, around 600 years before Jesus, the City of Jerusalem was in danger of falling to the Babylonians. "Give yourselves up", said Jeremiah, "this great City will fall". "Fall?" said the religious professionals, "Fall? Do you realise what our great prophet Isaiah said when the Assyrians attacked the City just over a century ago? Fall? This city cannot fall. God, through Isaiah, told us so." And religion had again made the professional error. It had rightly seen that God's revelation narrowed down to a particular channel, but had wrongly concluded that God would take the same line of approach the next time. It had correctly reckoned with God's faithfulness, but failed to understand His freedom. Jerusalem fell, as the alert Jeremiah had perceived.

The second example is from the time of the Early Christian Church, when the enthusiastic Saul journeyed on the Damascus Road. Unlike his predecessors in Jeremiah's time, the religiously zealous Saul was shaken out of his presupposed beliefs by the Word of the Living God, uttered this time through a blinding flash of light. Saul responded ... And ironically it was the so-called Christian believers' turn to doubt God's freedom; they could not comprehend that one so opposed to the Christian Faith could have been turned around 180 degrees. How utterly amazing is this God of surprises who, on the one hand, is faithful, but who, on the other hand, refuses to let us control His freedom.

**3. The Eagle Lands**

At Allen's Cross in Birmingham in the 1990's, the same – but totally different – thing happened. The Council Estate in that place was underprivileged by any standard, but through Kids Club Network and Jane Grinonneau, Associate Minister at Northfield Baptist Church, a Fun Club was started for the children of the area. This is what happened:

> One educated Church Member, finding the behaviour of the children in the Fun Club unacceptable, had been critical of the work. Out one day collecting for Christian Aid, she called at one of the many flats. The door opened and she was surprised to see a familiar little face (a Fun Club child) looking up at hers. With joy, the little girl rushed off and was heard to shout to her Mum, "It's my friend at the door!" The woman was moved to tears that the child should call her friend ... and she changed. In so many ways the children showed us how to be open, powerless, and free in the truth of Christ." (p.28)

Behold, the Eagle had Landed. Again. The Word of the Lord had struck at a time when, on this particular occasion, an "educated Church Member" expected nothing of the kind. Until the moment of Revelation, she was in control of the situation, and if the Word of the Lord was going to strike, it would be *from* her *to* the family rather than vice-versa. Who after all, ever heard of the Word of the Lord coming FROM the direction of such a home to the Christian Aid caller? Who, after reading their Isaiah scripture about inviolable Jerusalem, would have believed that a Word could come from someone who said that Jerusalem was not inviolable? Or who, after being called from their fishing trade to follow Jesus (Peter) would have believed that a Word could come from someone who persecuted the Christian Church (namely Saul)? But it can, and did, happen. The God of Jesus is the God who can be depended upon. He is faithful. But that does not mean that He will do things in the same way again and again. He is the Sovereign Lord who cannot be controlled by our religion. Now you see Him: now you don't.

Now, I don't know about you, but whenever I read "sovereign", I have a mental picture of someone like Henry V or Elizabeth I sitting on a throne, and that does not help my image of God. The artistic Christian images of Jesus ascending to be with His Father have not helped either, and in all this I have found it difficult to picture "sovereign" as "exempt from external control". To my mind, some novelists, playwrights, philosophers and artists are nearer to that dictionary definition of "sovereign" than are Elizabeth I or George VI. Not, you understand, that God has been pictured by all Christians as a traditional Queen or King; it is that the word "sovereign" is not very appropriate for God. Indeed, in the light of the control which modern day leaders exert over present monarchs, the term is inappropriate. Who after the death of Diana, Princess of Wales, could ever again believe that royalty was a fit image for God as the Sovereign God of freedom? The God and Father of Jesus is faithful. He is also exempt from external control. He is King. He is sovereign. The sovereignty and kingship, however, are almost everything we never associate with this world's Rulers.

"My Kingdom is NOT of this world," said Jesus, as if to emphasise the point. But it IS, says the same Jesus. Ahaa!

Though we must pause there for a moment. The Living God we worship as the God and Father of Jesus the Christ is one who may not be limited by others, but one who has limited Himself. The wonder or miracle of the God of Judaism and Christianity is that while He cannot be controlled by religion, in His freedom He has chosen to be controlled by His love for His human race. Exempt from external control, he is nevertheless free for us. And, as perfectly expressed by a modern hymn-writer, Brian Wren, to this God,

> "We strain to glimpse your mercy seat,
> And find you kneeling at our feet"

Faithful he might be; faithful indeed he is. But, for all that, He springs surprises; He is outside our control, and that, I would contend, is at once the blessing and the curse of prayer-book spirituality.

Prayer-book spirituality is at once a curse and a blessing; it reminds us that God is faithful, but deludes us into thinking that we have Him taped. Though here comes the crunch! We must go one step further. Is it that His "Revelatus" is from the poor upwards and because, despite 2000 years of reminders, we STILL talk about God being everywhere and think that the sugar-coating of his love is everywhere possible? This Father & Son redeeming combination is indeed a Limited Company, is indeed a Loving Company, but is it that He has not only confined knowledge of Himself to the human race, but restricted Himself to Revelatus through the downtrodden and marginalised of that family?

Great people of prayer, I sense, do not wish to give the impression that they can control God. But when one opens a prayer-book, the very opposite is the dangerous impression which one receives. And just as one turns on a tap to receive water for filling the kettle, so one senses that one will receive the Spirit of God when one prays in this way. Which is humbug. It ain't necessarily so! The Holy Spirit has a way of entering the situation through the back door and tapping (sic) the most unsuspecting person on the shoulder. Prayer-book spirituality is often helpful. To some extent it is necessary. Its beauty is that it can take the person who is praying outside of their usual tramlines. But it is dangerous. Protestors, non-conformists and rebels of many persuasions, from Amos, through Hosea, Isaiah, Jeremiah, Ezekiel, Jesus himself, Francis of Assisi, Julian of Norwich, Martin Luther and Martin Luther-King; Baptist, Primitive Methodist and especially Quaker, have said so.

## 4. The Dead God Resurrects

Indeed, in the 1960's a group of Christians, under the heading of "Death of God" tried desperately to express this tradition. They witnessed to the fact that the God who yesterday revealed himself there, is today found here. The One who reveals himself is the One who hides himself. You thought after Jenny that every time you went out into a garden to bury a pet cat you would hear an angel? Be gone. You had better look elsewhere. This God is seen in a storm. But then he is in the still, small voice and not in a storm at all. For Jeremiah he was in an almond tree, but when we come to look for him again in the same place, he is not there. As we say, it is like playing at Peek-a-boo, but with the stakes raised to infinite proportions.

We have mentioned the "Death of God" tradition, and although we have mentioned the 1960's in particular, the advocates of God's obituary are many and varied. We must defend those who infiltrated the Church 30 years ago. They did not believe that the Living God of Creation had ceased to be. Rather, they believed that our attempts to channel the Divine through prayers or other means were doomed to failure if we thought that by that means we could control God.

Earlier in the century, a much greater theologian, Karl Barth, made the same sort of protest with his attack upon religion. The "religion" to which he was referring was not everyone's definition of the same, and amongst his readership there have been endless arguments on what Barth meant by both the word and his attack upon it. But two things are certain; never has a follower of Christ emphasised as strongly as Barth both the paradox of the Sovereign God's being for the human race *and* the utter inability of the human race to reach to the heavens. The Living God, he said, cannot be controlled by us; He is free, but has made himself free for us. The way to understand this God is in Christ. But "Christ" is not a spiritual coating which anyone can add to their religious experience and think thereby it is the truth. It is not "Christ" as over against Buddha or Muhammed. In fact, this Christ is not spiritual at all. He is the Secular Christ (John Vincent) limited to flesh dimensions within a Gospel story. If we use the word "spiritual" here, it is co-terminous with being alongside the poor and marginalised of this too-fleshly world. In being free, Christ calls into question every religious venture which seeks to control God's freedom, including that of the Christian Church – not only the Mormon or Muslim packages are called into question, but the Methodist and Moravian too.

For all that, however, the Christ of the Gospel story is no less the Creator of the human mind, which pursues scientific analysis. He does not ask us to bury our heads in the sand. But we cannot by science fathom the Divine. Indeed, the scientific mind is free to pursue all aspects of religious phenomenon, and as Christians we can rejoice in such works as William James's great book *The Varieties of Religious Experience*. Like all scientific analysis, however, that only tells us what has happened; and unlike other areas of science, we are on dangerous ground if we try and create the conditions of experiment again in order to induce an approximate experience. The Revealed God is at the same time the Incognito God who in His Revelation to His human race is not at the mercy of the confines of a past Revelation. It is the same faithful God who Reveals Himself; of that we are sure. But his Revelation, whether through a burning bush, a sound of gentle stillness, a dream, or a flash of light at midday in the desert, cannot be manipulated and determined from our side. Nor can we reproduce it.

In the light of this, one is amazed that the Christian Church has fallen again and again for what I can only describe as the Religious Supermarket mentality. Reacting strongly against the "parrot fashion" nature of establishment worship, the early free-church enthusiasts began to list the experiences of the prophets and apostles, and sadly came to the conclusion that even though religious experiences were many and varied, what united them was their "religious" nature. They therefore concluded ("scientifically"!) that there was something religiously innate within every human being – a belief which is, indeed, the basis of the Quaker view of life. It was left to Karl Barth to question this most seriously. The call of the Living God to His human family is that in response to His faithfulness, it should be faithful to Him. There is nothing religious about it. Many verses of Scripture could be cited, but the most simple and most famous is that in Micah 6:8

> God has told you what is good;
> and what is it that the Lord asks of you?
> Only to act justly, to love loyalty.,
> to walk humbly before your God."

Some form of religious experience might await us. It is not to be ruled out, if by "religious" you mean a burning bush for Moses or a blinding flash of light for Saul. But we dare not seek it. Our job is to be faithful. Our job, as Jesus said to his disciples, is to follow Him. No religious experience on the shores of the sea of Galilee! No assurances from heaven for those who join His struggle. They might come later, but they must not be induced. We all belong to God because the Covenant He has made is with us all. He is our God. We, all of us, Jew and Gentile, black and white, Muslim and Moravian, male and female, evil and good, are One in Him. Our side of the Covenant agreement is to be the people he wants us to be, with or without Damascus Road.

But, but, but ... is there a clue to where we might find Him? Am I right to suggest – though only hesitatingly, you understand – that there is a place to be for following this God? Or better, to allow ourselves to be at His disposal? Might it be that this God who is for His human race, is not from the traditional monarch downwards, but from the marginalised upwards? Angels appeared at the tomb of the crucified. They appear after dogs have killed a cat. They appear on doorsteps in the reverse shock of Aid for professional Christians. Admittedly, the Kingdom of God Sign is not guaranteed at the margins, but it is worth looking there extra carefully.

Take the following, from Inderjit Bhogal:

> On week day mornings during school term, I like to walk with our two children, Liamarjit aged 8 and Anjuli aged 6, to school. At about 8.45 am the local streets are crowded with other parents, guardians and children. We reflect the community. We are black, Asian, white, young middle-aged, old. At one point on the journey, many of us have to cross a busy through road, Barnsley Road. At 8.45 am, the cars and buses and trucks are bumper to bumper both ways. Cyclists who brave the road, wear masks to cope with all the fumes. A lollipop lady assists those who wish to cross the road.
>
> As we wait at the pelican crossing, I look round and feel the thrill at the multi-cultural, multi-coloured, multi-religious group of women, men, boys and girls around me. In the midst of all the local concerns related to the many poor, the many religions, the many trees; in the midst of all the struggle in life we represent, we are a sign of the Kingdom of God which Jesus said is "in the midst of you". And I rejoice and give thanks to God.

> As I look around, I see also the faces of people looking out of buses and cars at us. Sometimes as they speed on, people turn their faces in the vehicles to look at us. But the looks are depressing. The faces show a sense of sheer resentment – the faces say something like: "I used to live there. Pitsmoor was a good place. Now it's over-ridden by all these "foreigners"".
>
> And they pass through. That's all they do now ... pass through – to town, to work, to homes elsewhere. They do not share my sense of delight at what I see. They only seem to deplore what they see. I want more people to rejoice with me, to see the city signs of the New Jerusalem, the Kingdom of God." (p.80)

I continually remind myself, as I remind my congregations, that my and their attendance at Sunday worship does not mean that we are any more precious in God's sight than the ruffian who climbed on the church roof during the week and stole the lead, or the one who sits in the public house drinking away his life. In fact, I say, we represent these people before God; we pray on their behalf. And this, I would maintain, is not to patronise them, nor to say that what we are doing is perfect.

I feel an overwhelming sense of privilege that, like Inderjit Bhogal, I have been given eyes to see the signs of God's Kingdom in some of the events around me. I might be wrong. I might be wrong to look more keenly for the signs among the poor. Others might be right in seeing them on a broader canvas. But my task is not to seek religious experience and, still less, put a religious veneer on everything that happens. I am part of the Human Race which is covenanted to Him. If I gather to worship, I gather to learn more from His Book about what He expects of me.

But again and again I find that book throwing up the poor as the unexpected place for His presence. May God, the Living God, forgive me that because of my job I too often get in the way of others seeing what I see. My professionalism is a terrible stumbling block. I cannot help it, of course, and the only way out would be to give in my notice and return to the pew. But that, if I am not too presumptuous, would be like Moses returning to the wilderness of his flock, or Saul returning to Tarsus. It can't be done, and if it could, it would not be too much use.

## 5. The Galilean Walks

Let none of us in privileged positions evade the following words, however. They come from John Vincent who has lived in the inner city of Sheffield for the past thirty years, and sensed the fact that the locals suspect the professionals, including the ministers. But occasionally the locals get to feel that they have the advantage over the professionals.

> Occasionally, the simple, down-to-earth stories of the happenings in the days of Jesus actually get through, and you can understand the stories even if not the sermons supposedly designed to explain or "preach on" them. Thus the inner city disciple occasionally hears of disciples being fishermen (Mk 1. 16-20), being called provincial Galileans (Acts 2.7), unlearned and ignorant (Acts 4.13). Or they hear of people asking in astonishment where Jesus got his teachings from (Mk 6.2), and wonder what happened to that tradition in the contemporary educated church.
>
> Or the urban disciple hears the frequent condemnations of his disciples uttered by Jesus (Mk 8. 17b-18 etc) and wonders why it was alright to be seriously eccentric in your faith then, but not now. Or he/she hears about a poor widow giving a tiny coin, proclaimed as having given more than some other wealthy donors (Mk 12. 41-44), and wonders why the Church today does well among the rich but pretty badly among the poor. Or she hears the story about the baby wrapped in swaddling clothes, lying in a manger (Lk 2.12), and wonders why single mothers out on the streets are not inside the churches. Or he hears that the temple offerings of Jesus' parents were those of the poorest (Lk. 2.24) and wonders why the pigeon-keepers seem so unwelcome now.
>
> Or, in Church, the inner city or housing estate Christian wonders why when a church leader comes, they are spoken to patronisingly, if the leader has to be as the servant (Mk 10. 42-45). Or why when the circuit or deanery is on parade, the small churches are introduced with a condescending smile, if, "Where two or three are gathered together, there is the Lord" (Mt 18.20). Or why, when the churches tell their stories, the tales of rich or successful churches are told, but not those of

poor or unsuccessful ones, if this is a community in which "the last shall be first and the first last" (Mk 9.35) (pp. 106-7).

From these experiences and many more like them, says John, "the inner city or housing estate Christian builds up a firm suspicion, based on repeated experiences of listening and participating, that whatever this story was about in the first place, it has got perverted by being adapted to the lifestyles, mindsets and vested interests of professional, middle class Christians, and a generally status quo view of society, largely indistinguishable from that of everyone else in the surrounding society".

Is there then a way of being free for the God who is free for us?

More sharply, are the manner, places, people and events of Jesus' being free for us, as recorded in the Gospels, suggestive of the manner, places, people and events of Jesus' being free for us, in our own world today? Do the manner and specifics of the Word become flesh suggest, or even determine, contemporary epiphanies - or revelations? Has the Deus Absconditus become more predictable after Jesus? How far has God now limited His sovereign freedom, now that He has appeared to us in His prophet Jesus, the definitive Word?

Or, when we claim that our faith must be Christ-centred, must we not take that absolutely seriously? Or, to put it more sharply still, after Jesus, has the Deus Absconditus escaped every avenue other than that of the poor?

And does the Angel tap, the Eagle land and the Dead God resurrect in the places and the people and the happenings where the Galilean walks?

# Ian Fraser

# A SPIRITUALITY OF RESISTANCE

## 1. The Call to Resist.

This world order is to become the order of our Lord and of his Christ (Rev. 11.15). We are to share in that "becoming" in partnership with God, setting up signs of the Kingdom (life structured God's way) here and now, to anticipate its fullness beyond the here and now. The requirement that we "offer our bodies as a living sacrifice" includes the, costly if need be, confrontation of the present order in order to turn it into God's order. Jesus Christ fought structures which humiliated and crushed human beings. He came that all might have life and have it abundantly.

We are called to follow in his way. Theology provides resources for transforming the cosmos with God. Life is entrusted to us to spend in that service. Concrete tasks are indicated.

It is as "God's servant" (Rom. 13.4) that government has a right to exercise power. It can go bad and forfeit that right (Rev. 13). Then we should obey God rather than men, as Peter and John did in Acts 4. Pilate had Jesus in his power. But for that power to be exercised with genuine authority, Pilate would have needed to recognise its "from above" nature. Even when authority is validly conferred in some judicial structure it is not authenticated until it is recognised and acknowledged as being the genuine article.

---

**Ian Fraser is a long-time missioner, theologian and writer of the Iona Community now based at Scottish Churches House, Dunblane. The present article was written during the Poll Tax Campaign.**

Emergent authority, such as John the Baptist's, can be recognised and acknowledged though it lies outside the traditional structures. Accordingly, governmental authority lies not simply in the ability to get things done ("dunamis") – an elective dictatorship can ensure that. To have genuine authority, its policies need to be acknowledged to be just and appropriate. A reminder of the "from beyond" character of genuine authority can be provided on earth by e.g. parliament, church and people. Though the final reference in England and Wales is to parliament, in Scotland it is to the people, but, together with church, they hold responsibility for challenging actions done on a mere "power to effect" basis. When, to get Poll Tax legislation through, Lords were dug out of the backwoods, cobwebs brushed off them, and they were directed through the Lobby in wheelchairs and returned to Rip Van Winkle Country, we get a clear signal that the legislation has a power base but lacks an authority base.

Calvin (Lecture XIII) said "Because earthly princes forfeit all their power when they revolt against God ... we should resist them rather than obey." Knox, before Mary Queen of Scots, spoke of "the right of the subject to disobey where the ruler contravenes the law of God." How are we to test what comes into "revolt against God" and the "law of God"? I would say that the Fathers gave two guides: a) where the poor are crushed instead of given place and protection; b) where idolatry, especially of riches, is encouraged – Christians and others are called to resist.

## 2. A Spirituality of Resistance

I so often hear the concept of spirituality restricted to prayer and the devotional life. It must be related to all the points at which our spirits strive with God's spirit seeking life for the world. It covers hearing of cries; the depth and quality of response; capacity for discernment, resilience and availability; concern for the neighbour; and a readiness to muck in. Since the Holy Spirit's concern is for the whole world, the command to be alert and stay awake and to help others to be equally watchful lest we be taken off guard when a day of decision comes, is addressed to all.

At the exodus from Egypt, it is made clear that God hears the cries of his people – God hears cries, not just prayers (as, on the Day of Judgement, it is what nations live, not what they profess, that counts). The Spirit strives with our spirits, who do not know what to pray for; and intercedes with us, in accordance with God's will, with groans that words cannot express (Rom. 8. 26,27). Spirituality has to do with a wrestling in which the inarticulateness of cries and responses is no barrier, because it is not the capacity to get things sorted out rationally which is decisive, but a faithful wrestling to live in imaginative obedience to God's will.

Spirituality concerns the depth, the rooting of our action and reflection. This includes awareness of our own sinfulness and our share in the world's sinfulness, a readiness to be instructed differently in relation to actions (should I continue my refusal to pay the Poll Tax if local services are badly cut back?), a trust in God to draw what we do well into a creative purpose and to cover what is ill done with a comprehending and a comprehensive forgiveness. Life is to be rooted in God's life.

1. The gift of Discernment is central. This includes:

> Research: we have to be serious about God's dynamically developing creation and what faces us in the slice of time and space in which life is entrusted to us. E.g. Senator Salonga in the Philippines spoke to me of the "evangelical necessity of research into transnational companies lest the world get into a powerful grasp which is other than God's". We must do our homework on "the situation" as on "the revelation".
>
> Prayer: the mind of the Spirit must be strenuously and quietly sought;
>
> Selection follows from research and prayer: i.e. availability to the Spirit to discern among all that could be done, what is at this point commanded;
>
> Timing: Jesus was timed through his mission like a boxer from his corner: "Suss out the situation"/"get in some telling blows"/"husband your strength"/"in for the kill". Decisions to go to Jerusalem secretly or very publicly were a matter of timing to suit the Father's strategy. Flailing fists, every round, are not on.
>
> Alongsidedness. For poor people confused and fearful, acting as a Mackenzie friend is a sign of spiritual awareness. When I asked Hong Kong street-traders why, being unbelievers, they had such words of praise for the Christian Industrial Mission, they simply said "When the police harass us, who comes between us and the police? When we are taken to court, who is beside us in court?"

2. Resilience. Spirituality has that in it which can deal with blows and set-backs. Craig's catechism in the 1560's has something like this:

> Q. "Who are the saints of God?"
> A: "Those who, trusting to Christ, often fall and fail; but, by his grace, pick themselves up, dust themselves down and soldier on."

3. Spirituality is developed normally in community; though people in solitary confinement (prison or vows) are not excluded: it is in the communion of saints that they make growth. A spirituality for resistance can mark whole communities and the persons who make up these. Growth comes from building one another up in love.

4. Spirituality trusts God's action in the incarnation. As Jesus demanded no life which allowed ideal choices, neither should we. It has been a weakness of Christians to wait for clean, clear situations so that actions may clearly spring from a faith-basis. Jesus accepted life-as-it-is with all its muddy unclarities and uncertainties, and worked out our salvation. Trembling on the brink can go on for ever. Waiting for the "right time" can be disobedience.

5. Through reliance on the Spirit there can come that alertness which a) allows people to see afar off what consequences may stem from present actions; or b) allows what may come out of the blue disconcertingly: so that vulnerable human beings may be prepared, and have a chance to stand, not fall.

Inderjit Bhogal

# PRAYER, PROTEST AND POLITICS

## 1. Political Holiness

I walked from the Town Hall in Sheffield to 10 Downing Street to hand deliver a letter to the Prime Minister, asking for changes in the rules so that Asylum Seekers who are not convicted of crime are not held in prisons. Posting the letter would have been cheaper and easier. The walk underlined the depth of my concern. Imprisoning Asylum Seekers not convicted of crime illustrated clearly the injustices enshrined within British Immigration and Asylum laws. Others are held in detention centres. Those who are not detained are criminalised too by being defined as "bogus" or "illegal immigrants", and by being deprived of support. Current proposals (1999) threaten to be even stricter, not fairer. The policies have helped to create an environment in which black people generally are targets of abuse and attack. There is a place for holy anger, I needed to express mine with grace. I walked. The walk was a pilgrimage of prayer and protest. It was a holy and political act. The action had a greater effect than sealing and sending a letter by post.

When I met Desmond Tutu – there was no need for him to speak. His actions spoke for him before he opened his mouth. I had seen him confront South African military armed to their teeth, with a Bible in his hands. He was protesting at the Government declaration that the Church must not speak out on political issues. Tutu – the Gospel cannot be silenced.

---

**Inderjit Bhogal is Director of the Urban Theology Unit in Sheffield. A Methodist Minister, he is also part-time Minister at the Upper Wincobank Undenominational Chapel.**

He is clearly a Christian who is not afraid of political action that is inspired by the Gospel. Holiness shines from him. And people respond to such holiness. He is an inspiration to Christians, to people of all faiths and to people who profess no particular faith.

People like him and M. L. King, Oscar Romero and M. K. Ghandi have been an inspiration to me. I have become engaged in all kinds of political activity, for example

- Marched against National Front
- Stood with bread strikers and coal miners on strike
- Supported Greenham Common Women's protest, and CND
- Stood with "rioters" in Handsworth
- Marched with those who protested at police violence and racism
- Marched with students against freezing of grants
- Held vigils with anti poll tax campaigners
- Lobbied politicians for homeless people
- Walked to protest at detention of Asylum Seekers unfairly held, and visited people in Detention Centres.

Why?

- I am for life:- It is God's desire for all to have life in all its abundance
- I am for truth:- Christians need to expose falsehood and bear witness to all aspects of truth:- And to facilitate the telling of stories of truth
- I am for justice:- This is a basic Biblical demand
- I am for mercy:- We are called to be merciful and to show mercy as God is merciful.

There is a long tradition of Christian political witness, and Christian Socialism. This is well documented. What has been missing has been the willingness of Christian political activists to express the spirituality or the holiness of their political action. Perhaps this is because spirituality and holiness have been hijacked by those who have defined it narrowly in terms of negation and rejection of life, and separation from life. Spirituality has certainly been hijacked by nice retreat centres situated away from inner-cities, in the hills and by the sea. There are those who will have nothing to do with such holiness and spirituality.

In this reflection I want to look briefly at Biblical insights into holiness and some insights that emerge from Christian action.

## 2. Holiness in Scripture

### Holiness as Separation

There is a strand within scripture where Israel's call to holiness is a demand for separation: "You are holy to me because I, the Lord, am holy, and I have set you apart from the nations to be my own." (Lev. 20 : 26). God is seen in this strand as holy and separate from all that is considered to be common and profane. Anything that is considered to be unclean, or defiled cannot come near God. And so God's people are required to be separate from all people, practices and objects that can defile. God's people are required to keep themselves from all impurity. Individuals and indeed the whole nation are called to be holy in this sense. In this understanding the call to holiness is all embracing: socially, psychologically, sexually, spiritually, ethnically, politically and so on. No realm of human existence is excluded.

People erred from this call to Holiness. Judgement came in the form of Exile. In fact, it was in Exile that the religious leaders reasoned that it was their deviation from holiness that had brought this particular punishment. Exile brought its own complications. The call to separation from other people was frustrated.

Upon return from Exile, it was noted by priests like Ezra and Nehemiah that while some people had learned what holiness meant, others had defiled themselves by marrying foreigners. In Ezra 10, we are told that all who had married foreigners had to send their partners back to Babylon. The sin of such an unholy alliance was so grave that all culprits are named. Writers of books like Ruth and Jonah challenged such attitudes and actions. The Post-Exilic community's political strategy was the infusion of holiness into the nation. The move to separation was reaffirmed. This was the politics of holiness.

In the Inter-Testamental times, other variations to this programme developed. For some it was not enough that the nation was separate from other nations. Extreme groups like the Essenes emerged. They sought separation not only from other nations, but also from their own people who were considered to be impure. You could only be considered to be holy in this group understanding if you were 'one of us'. Scriptural holiness was now a matter of drawing the boundaries. The standards became stricter and stricter, to the point that some groups, like the Essenes, drew apart completely to live in remote communities. They required others to adhere to their standards.

In the New Testament, we are presented with some of the disputes of those who considered themselves to be pure and holy. The disputes cover such issues as ritual purity, Sabbath observance, fasting, tithing, the company Jesus wined and dined with, circumcision, the relationships with Gentiles, Hellenists and Samaritans, and Sinners.

**Holiness as Closeness**

Into a world with clear boundaries, and distinctions between who is holy and who is a sinner, came Jesus, who ate with sinners and tax collectors, proclaimed good news to the poor, announced the Kingdom of God, called men and women to repentance and a life marked by mercy, forgiveness, love and service. Jesus, too, advocated the politics of holiness.

Jesus cared deeply for the state of the nation and demonstrated this by;

- Breaking down the boundaries;
- Proclaiming that God's love is not restricted by boundaries, and comes close to people;
- Including those who have been excluded.
- Eating with anyone who would eat with him.

Everything Jesus did and said demonstrated these things. Let me use just one chapter from the Gospels to illustrate.

Matthew 15 includes the story of the healing of the Canaanite woman's daughter, and a meal with a large crowd. These stories are set in the context of one of the disputes about purity and defilement. The chapter begins with questions about food and ends with a meal. By placing here the stories about Jesus and a Canaanite woman and a communal meal, Matthew shows Jesus engaging in activities which, on one understanding of holiness, could defile a person. As a man, he is shown speaking with a woman, as a Nazarene, he is shown meeting with a Canaanite, as a man of one particular faith he is shown in dialogue with a person of another faith. He even commends faith that has matured outside a given territory. Matthew, who tends to be more chauvinistic and nationalistic than the other Gospel writers, shows Jesus transcending all these barriers. Then he writes that Jesus, "moved with compassion for the crowd", organised and prepared and provided a meal for them all.

The disputes regarding purity and defilement continue of course into the life of the early church. Before his encounter with the Gentile Cornelius, Peter is challenged by God: "What God has called clean, you must not call profane."

(Acts 10 : 15). Peter later says "God has shown me that I should not call anyone profane or unclean" (Acts 10 : 28). He repeats these words to the Apostles (Acts 11 : 9). The words are repeated three times, which suggests that they are critically important. We know however that Peter, pillar in the Church that he was, found this a difficult lesson to learn. In Galatians 2, we are told of an incident where Peter is happy eating with Gentiles, outsiders. However, when Christians of the "Circumcision faction" (Gal 2 : 12) arrived, he withdrew and "kept himself separate". We read that some of his companions "joined him in this hypocrisy, so that even Barnabas was led astray by their hypocrisy" (Gal 2 : 13). Paul writes that when this happened he opposed Peter "face to face" (Gal 2 : 11) seeing that he and companions "were not acting consistently with the truth of the Gospel" (Gal 2 : 14).

So, we have at least two different notions of holiness within scripture. One is the demand to separate, because God is holy and separate. One is the call to crossing boundaries and to connectedness, because God is a God who is close and not far away. In the one concept people speak of holy things and profane things, and never the two shall meet. The other concept is summed up in the incarnation and in the words of God to Peter, repeated three times: "what God has made clean, you must not call profane." These words were related to animals in the first instance; Peter later broadens them to include "anyone" (Acts 10 : 28).

## 3. Separatism or Connectedness?

Both of these understandings of holiness are scriptural. There is clearly a debate and sometimes dispute between the two strands. Both the understandings of holiness have been handed down through the ages, and are evident in church life today. They surface in church debates on sex, sexuality, gender, race, religious diversity, politics and so on.

There are those who today see holiness in terms of clean and unclean, pure and impure, who call for clearer boundaries and lines to be drawn, and demand separation, and state this quite categorically as scriptural holiness. The emphasis here is also on personal holiness, and sometimes this can obscure the political consequences of holiness. This line has almost monopolised the understanding of holiness. It is a line incidentally that finds support in other faith traditions. This approach, though, explains to some extent the paucity of reflection on political holiness within the sphere of Christian Socialism and political action. It makes people nervous, almost, and reluctant to speak about spirituality or holiness, which are seen so much as effected through escape from the world rather than through engagement with the world.

We do have Christian reflection on political holiness. See for example, *True Prayer,* by Kenneth Leech, and indeed all his work; and *Praying the Kingdom – towards a Political Spirituality,* by Charles Elliott. Christians in the so-called Third World, however, have the greatest riches to offer in terms of political holiness. The best example in my view is *Spirituality of Liberation* by Jon Sobrino. From Northern Ireland has also emerged this year, within the environment of ceasefires and peace agreement, a document entitled *The Politics of Holiness*, by Alwyn Thomas. It is published by the Evangelical Contribution on Northern Ireland (ECONI). It is an excellent and timely contribution coming out of a time when people who have experienced what separation and boundaries can do to communities are talking about breaking down the boundaries, building relationships, and accommodating more people in their world. I am indebted to all the texts I have listed.

In our contemporary world of ethnic cleansing, in which people say to others "I can't live with you because you are different", we need holiness that calls people to follow through Jesus' actions today, and:

- Break down boundaries;
- Proclaim God who knows no boundaries and who is close to people;
- Include those who are excluded;
- Eat food with all those who will eat with them, and to work and pray to ensure that all have bread.

John Wesley called for "social holiness". The best Methodist expression of such holiness, or any holiness that is to be relevant today could in fact be characterised by a word we should not lose sight of: Connexion. This word represents the opposite of separation. It speaks of relatedness, and of interdependence. It is a recognition that if we are to understand the world church, and indeed the whole created order today, then we must acknowledge that everything and everyone is connected, more joined together than we ever realised before. The word of Jesus, "Let no one separate those who God has joined together" should not be confined only to human matrimony.

A reflection on Politics today, Connexity, by Geoff Mulgan, states that "Connectedness will dominate the lives of our children and grandchildren. The connections spreading around us are only a foretaste of what is to come. Even today, more than a century after its invention, less than half the world's population has access to a telephone and little more than one percent of all households use the Internet. Soon, the combination of a rapid rise in the world's population, continuing advances in technology and sharply falling communication costs will make the world a far more interconnected place than it is today" (p. 3)... "Our primary responsibility today is to find ways to live with interdependence, not deny it" (p. 10). Another document from N Ireland, *Sectarianism*, puts it like this: We must find ways of "living together in difference without wanting to dominate, destroy or separate" (p. 40).

The most outstanding novel of the 1990's *God of Small Things* by Arundathi Roy is a story about people who live in very different worlds, risking a relationship of intimacy. With all our differences, this is the challenge that faces us in terms of holiness and politics: to move from sectarianism and separatism to connectedness and relationships of trust, reciprocity and respect. The way forward for us all could be through holiness. However we understand holiness, the ultimate test would be that given by Jesus. "By their fruits you shall know" true disciples, he said. The fruits of the Spirit come together to manifest Christian maturity and holiness.

**4. Holiness as the Need of Church Today**

Holiness has also been long considered to be contained within, or restricted to, particular wings of the church. Those outside them are considered to be heretical. Division into various groups is a feature of church life today, as at any time in church history. Each group claims to be truly or most authentically church. The divisions can be bitter and can be an assault on the very basis of Christian life.

Jon Sobrino in *Spirituality of Liberation* p. 9-10 argues that the solution to this situation calls for a "spirit of holiness". The way groups usually try to tackle division is by an appeal to orthodoxy or the power of theological reasoning. There are those who try to justify their exclusive claims to truth by appealing to pure orthodoxy. There are those who will appeal to the gospel, and to theology more in tune with the gospel. So there is a conflict between authority and the power of theological reasoning. Sobrino argues that the real challenge facing us in this context is not the need to wrestle with the problem of the identity of the true church. His desire is to add an additional element to the discussion – namely, that, "when all is said and done, the stamp of approval of any ecclesial group claiming to be the true church can only be the holiness of that group." Whoever truly loves the church and desires its renewal; whoever wishes to assist the church in this period of confusion, uncertainty and division "must be ready to bear the witness of holiness. It would be an error to confuse love for the church with an outrageously exaggerated defence of institution and orthodoxy. But it would likewise be insufficient – not wrong, but insufficient – to wish to demonstrate one's love for the church only by way of correct theological argumentation ... Ultimately only holiness counts. And only holiness sheds the light of credibility on the truth or argument."

## 5. Bert Bissell

Bert Bissell, blessed soul that he was, died on 2 November 1998, All Soul's Day, within All Saintstide; and, remarkably, his funeral was held on 10 November, so close to Armistice Day. In the days he was fit and well, he climbed Ben Nevis within this week. Appropriately, his body was buried at the foot of Ben Nevis, in Glen Nevis, on 13 November.

At his home in Dudley, the front room contains a remarkable collection of memorabilia. One of these is a painting that shows an old man at prayer in a chapel. That's Bert Bissell. A man of prayer. However else he is remembered, let him be remembered as a man of prayer, a deeply spiritual, saintly man. Everything he did and achieved needs to be seen in this context.

- Leading a Bible Class for nearly 80 years;
- Walking almost a million miles, many times to tops of mountains in England, Wales, Ireland, Scotland, Switzerland, Australia, S Africa.
- The forging of international relationships especially with Hiroshima, Japan.
- Sending peace messages to the moon, the sea and to many mountains.
- Loyalty to football clubs like Coventry City and Dudley Town.
- Being Dudley's first Probation Officer ...

And so much more for which he was awarded the MBE and the World Methodist Peace Prize. All this has to be seen in the context of prayer and spirituality. Bert Bissell did not divide his living into sections of sacred and spiritual. His whole life was one great connected chain of prayer. He was a holy man .. a guru.

Holiness of the quality that shone from Bert is in short supply today. "By their fruits you shall know" true disciples, said Jesus. All the fruits of the Spirit come together to form the holiness that we saw in Bert Bissell. It was a holiness immersed in life, not detached from it.

In all the challenges facing the church today, with all our confusions, conflicts and divisions, uncertainties and fears, Bert Bissell, and others like him, show us that people respond to holiness. Holiness is the need of all faiths, and of people who profess no particular faith but are deeply spiritual. There is an insatiable desire, at the turn of the millennium, for qualities of holiness and saintliness.

## 6. Holiness in Prayer, Protest and Politics

It was Karl Barth who wrote: "To clasp the hands in prayer is the beginning of an uprising against the disorder of the world." Jesus taught us to say, when we pray, "Your Kingdom come".

My claim to fame is that the Sheffield Telegraph once used something I said as their quote of the week; "Prayer and politics go hand in hand." Prayer and politics are often considered to be different and separate realities not just because they are but because they ought to be. More and more it is being acknowledged in Christian circles that this is a false distinction, and an unrealistic hope. The struggles to link faith and politics, prayer and social action are seen to be compatible.

In spite of the words of Romans 13.1 "Let everyone be subject to authority, for there is no authority that is not ordained by God", the church throughout the world, in the 20th century at least, has been prepared to take action and speak out against state injustice, interrogation and terrorism. The church has recognised that "authorities" can by tyrannical and dictatorial, a factor that Romans 13 fails to take account of. And the church has been prepared to challenge and protest at tyranny and dictatorship, choosing when there is a conflict to "obey God rather than man". We recognise that sometimes the church has done this reluctantly, and only when pushed. In a book called *Gandhi the Man*, the author Eknath Easwaran, argues that, during the struggles for freedom from oppression in S Africa, a Hindu, Gandhi, reminded Christians of the way Jesus wished them to live. Martin Luther King, Janani Luwum, Oscar Romero, Dietrich Bonhoeffer and others like them are honoured as Christian martyrs who led Christians to resist and to protest at state injustice and oppression in USA, Uganda, El Salvador, Germany and so on. Christian Socialism has a long history in this country, and is well documented in Chris Bryant's book, *Possible Dreams*. In Methodism, we have an honourable history of political engagement recently through people like Pauline Webb and Paul Boateng, and through Conference protesting with "outrage" and "anger" at issues such as poverty and unjust detention of asylum seekers. One of the most remarkable symbols of political action and protest by Christians in the UK was when 60,000 people of all ages and abilities and many national backgrounds formed a human chain around Birmingham on 16 May at the G8 meeting. They went to express outrage and anger that one billion people live on the verge of death because of debt, and because of our lifestyle. The Jubilee 2000 campaign to end debt has gained considerable support and will be sustained.

"Those in Britain who try to tell the Church to keep out of political issues are asking us to unlearn the most painful and expensive lessons which Christianity has had to learn in this century", John Davies in *The Crisis the Cross,* p. xiv. We have much to learn still and the building blocks of injustice remain. Britain is still characterised by inequality and insecurity. The world remains divided between those who are rich and those who are poor, between black and white, Christians and Muslims, and so on. Religious traditions have often sanctioned such divisions and accompanying atrocities.

What I am concerned about is not whether prayer and politics can be partners. I have no doubt about their relationship. What I am concerned about is whether politics is failing those who remain on what is considered to be the margin of society; whether politics can catch up with the Biblical agenda of justice; and whether the church has the nerve and the will at the turn of the millennium to put politics under the spotlight of the Gospel of Jesus Christ.

What is the line of the church, for example, in a state where innocent asylum seekers are kept detained in prison or prison conditions for many months before even being brought to trial?

Where would we find Jesus in our own society and political systems? Surely he would take sides with those on the margins!

Prayer and politics go hand in hand. The topic is often debated. The case for their relationship is well made. But what about holiness and politics? The question emerges out of the relationship between prayer and politics. For many Christian people the context for Christian maturity and for holiness is political action. As Jon Sobrino says, holiness requires politics, and politics requires holiness.

## 7. Holiness Requires Politics

For me, holiness is rooted in response to God. And my response is rarely voluntary. I am usually "compelled" to take a certain course of action, a bit like Simon of Cyrene. He had gone along to see what all the fuss was about, he was a spectator, a bystander, looking on. He was compelled to carry the cross. Compel is a better word than call. Compel suggests being pushed or driven into certain direction or action. Call hints at a beckoning. JV Taylor in *The Go-Between God* suggests that the work of the Holy Spirit of God is to draw attention to the beckoning of God.There is an element of that. But the Holy Spirit also drives people into certain ways. Jesus was driven by the Holy Spirit into the wilderness after his baptism.

God wants all people to have life in all its fullness. The vision of God is portrayed in Scripture as everyone having a home, with a garden, and with a tree in the garden. This is the Biblical image of Shalom. It is God's will that people should have the freedom and resources to "build houses and live in them, plant vines and eat their fruit" (Isa. 65.21). For this to be achieved, everything that prevents it should be brought to an end, such as poverty, debts, enslavement, exploitation of land.

When we are compelled to take political action, the resulting impact on lifestyle can be the arena, the crucible in which holiness grows. The quality of holiness that in particular deepens, is that of holy anger and mercy. Jesus is driven to cleanse the temple of unjust exploitation by anger; he is said to have snorted with the snorting of horses when he is confronted with leprosy and disease; he is moved with mercy for the crowd that is hungry (Mt. 15. 32).

This anger and mercy can be seen in the prophetic action and words of those who expose the truth of the world as it is. Prophets are not those who foretell what is to come, but those who forthtell, speak of the truth that stares people in the face but which people choose to turn a blind eye or a deaf ear to in the present.

When anger and mercy come together in prophetic action and words, there is a clear requirement for metanoia, for repentance, for things to change, for people to turn their direction so that life in all its abundance is accessible to all.

Anger and mercy require careful thought, and effective action and words. Nothing less than a thorough exposing and unmasking of scandal and falsehood and an uncovering and announcing of truth will be satisfactory.

The politics of anger and mercy will be conducted in solidarity with those who are the most victimised, the most vulnerable, the most powerless.

The question is raised whether holiness expressed in political acts of anger and mercy may support violent action. There is a long history of debate on this matter. I believe that in today's world with weapons of mass destruction and indiscriminate weapons, the doctrine of Just War is not adequate any more. Nor is the doctrine of Just Revolution. People like Mahatma Gandhi, Martin Luther King and Desmond Tutu have shown ways to confront the might and monstrosity of state terror and victimisation with the non-violence of truth, anger and mercy. We must find ways to resolve conflict in peaceful ways.

But as we have seen in the lives of the martyrs, those Christians who engage in political action, even when this is tempered with anger and mercy, are persecuted, demonised and murdered. The Christian martyrs are growing in number; the more recent ones have been Bishop Joseph in Pakistan who accepted martyrdom to highlight the persecution of Christians in Pakistan; and Bishop Juan Gerardi Conedera of Guatemala who was assassinated in mysterious circumstances two days after he launched a report denouncing human rights abuses in his country.

Jon Sobrino in *Spirituality of Liberation* (p. 83) has written: "If the spilt blood of so many bishops, priests, nuns, catechists, teachers, and also Christians who are peasants, workers, trade unionists and combatants, is not a convincing argument that the political is a proper sphere for holiness, and moreover that at the moment holiness normally means involvement in politics, then there is no theological discourse that could be convincing. Those who are not convinced, even by the clearest examples, are unable to interpret Jesus' death as the death of the Just One. They would be left with the alternative of interpreting his death as that of a blasphemer and subversive, as the powers of his time wanted it to be understood." So, the holiness, mercy and anger inevitably require political action. John Wesley reminds us that "there is no holiness but social holiness".

**8. Politics Requires Holiness**

It is true also that politics requires holiness (Sobrino, p. 84-85). Politics is exhausting and demanding. It requires space for solitude and silence, prayer and meditation. Political action such as a walk seeking a fair deal for asylum seekers in detention, or any action for racial justice, can be dismissed as purely a political activity if it is not rooted in and motivated by Biblical and Gospel values of equality, justice, mercy, freedom and dignity. Christian political action is part of our spiritual discipline and pilgrimage. Our political action, then, should not be divorced from prayer and worship. Racial Justice Sunday, for example, is not about confining work and prayer for racial justice to one day in the year. Rather it provides an opportunity to root our commitment to racial justice in prayer, worship and fasting. It encourages us to see that praying, protesting and petitioning go hand in hand. It offers an opportunity to make liturgy the environment in which, along classic lines of worship, we can:

- Affirm our conviction that we are all made in the image of God, black and white.
- Name the sin of racism, acknowledge our own complicity, and repent and seek forgiveness.
- Proclaim that Christ came to save us <u>all</u>.
- Proclaim and state the patterns for new ways of living and loving that rejoice in diversity.
- Pray for victims of racism and for all those who work for right relationships and racial justice
- Covenant, offer ourselves, our gifts, including money, for racial justice.
- Commission people to go forth in the name of Christ to work and pray for racial justice.

Latin American Bishops, meeting in Puebla, stated quite categorically that Christian involvement in politics is a way of rendering worship to God. The central Christian act of worship is the Eucharist, a sacramental meal in which we give thanks for Jesus and his living, giving and loving. His lifestyle created a new and life-giving, empowering politics. As we eat and drink at the Eucharist, we are nourished and awakened to the fact that millions have no food, and no clean water to drink. As we celebrate the life of Christ, we are awakened to the fact that millions live on the verge of death, and have no life. The Eucharist becomes a subversive meal, as it was for Jesus and his friends. As they ate, they spoke of betrayal.

The Eucharist celebrates equality, and offers bread and drink to all, and anticipates a time when all shall sit at the heavenly banquet and eat and drink. Wherever people are told there is no place for them, no food and drink for them, the no becomes "an insult to the holiness of God and his justice. The 'no' is a death sentence emitted daily on millions". (Frank Regan SSC in *Vocation for Justice,* Spring 1998).

Our politics and political action require holiness also if they are to be sustained and not squashed under pressure. They require nurturing, maturing, deepening holiness. Our political action requires the constant reminder that God is on our side and alongside us when we rage for justice. I noted the words of Desmond Tutu on 8 June 1980 when he was speaking on the programme "Heart of the Matter". He said, "We keep saying 'please choose to be on the winning side' because we are the winning side. God is on our side, not because we are good, or better, but because he is the God of liberation; and we will not forget who assisted us in becoming free."

Politics needs holiness also to keep all of us who engage in political action from all the temptation that goes with it. And don't we know about it. "By their fruits you shall know them" is the spiritual and ethical criterion in the realm of politics as anywhere else. Anyone who is engaged in politics can be tempted to exchange the collective cause for the individual's own causes. Instead of seeking the welfare of the poorest, you promote your own cause. In the place of serving people, you can end up dominating and manipulating people. Instead of seeking truth, you can be overtaken by the need to spread propaganda. Instead of seeking equality, you can end up displaying moral and racist supremacy.

Sobrino says "We need the Spirit of Jesus in political action and in those areas that have most to do with politics. We need purity of heart to see the truth of things, to analyse successes and failures and plans for liberation, to keep as a criterion for action what will most benefit the poor majorities, to overcome the temptation to dogmatism, to which it is easy to succumb in all political activity. We need to seek peace even in the midst of struggle without turning to violence, ... into a kind of mysticism, and without placing all our confidence in it to resolve objective problems and neglecting other more peaceful forms of struggle... We need pity so that we do not relativise disproportionately the people's pain and reduce it to an unavoidable social cost, so that we do not close off the future from the enemy, so that we do not suppress the difficult possibility of forgiveness and reconciliation. We need humility to know that fundamentally we are 'unprofitable servants', sinners, so that in action we remain grateful, in difficulty we ask for help, and we do the work of liberation as forgiven sinners."

This is the holiness that political action demands if it is to remain and grow in love. There are political saints. They are the ones who identify with the poorest and most vulnerable, and who take risks of faith. People need holiness in politics, and politics rooted in and inspired by holiness. Political holiness may help the church to retain its credibility if the church can commit resources to the exposing of social scandal and the announcing of truth as the foundation of its life, mission, witness and worship. If the church can do this it may be able to "face the challenge to the future of faith when other struggles for the salvation of (people) are undertaken by those who do not act in the name of Jesus Christ." (Sobrino, p.86)

## 9. Concluding Comments

- We need to acknowledge that people experience difficulty with prayer, and are looking for help in this area.

- Prayer is not just about kneeling and seeking the intervention of a remote, heavenly deity. It is political action because it is about transforming the world.

- Holiness is whatever produces the totality of Jesus, and particularly his anger and mercy in people.

- Holiness is wholeness.

- God is political and acts in history.

We need to integrate prayer, protest and holiness in politics.

---

Bibliography

A.K.M. Adams, **What is Postmodern Biblical Criticism?** Fortress, 1995
Chris Bryant, **Possible Dreams**, Hodder & Stoughton, 1996
John Davies, **The Crisis the Cross**, Canterbury Press, 1997
Eknath Easwaran, **Gandhi the Man**, Nilgiri Press, 1978
Charles Elliott, **Praying the Kingdom – Towards a Political Spirituality**, DLT, 1985.
Kenneth Leech , **True Prayer**, Sheldon, 1980
Geoff Mulgan, **Connexity**, Vantage Press, 1998
Frank Regan SSC, **Vocation for Justice**, Spring 1998
Arundathi Roy, **The God of Small Things**
Jon Sobrino, **Spirituality of Liberation – Towards Political Holiness**, (Orbis, 1988, 3rd Printing,1990)
John Spong, **Why Christianity must Change or Die**, Harper, 1998.
R.S. Sugitharajah, **Voices from the Margin**, SPCK, 2nd Ed, 1998
**Sectarianism**, Irish Inter-Church Meeting, 1993
J.V. Taylor, **The Go-Between God**, SCM Press, 1983
Alwyn Thomson, **The Politics of Holiness**, ECONI, 1998, p. 22.
Methodist Conference Report on Authority, 1998

# Jan Royan

# A SPIRITUALITY FOR INNER CITY VOCATION

For those of us who live and work in inner cities, having a spirituality which is relevant and resourcing is essential. I came to Sheffield nine years ago from the Lake District where I had lived in a cottage surrounded by fields and sheep, with views of a lake and the fells, where just walking the dog gave a spiritual uplift. At first I found it hard to find God in the inner city among derelict steelworks, shabby and vandalised buildings and rubbish-strewn streets. But as always, God dwells with God's people everywhere and anywhere. And it is through the people with whom I have rubbed shoulders, with whom I worked and with whom I worshipped, that God was most often revealed to me. It was not a God of green fields and spectacular beauty, but it was and is a God of humour, resilience and diversity, with odd glimpses of beauty.

I believe that we are linked to God and to each other through our spirituality. The words we use to explore and explain our beliefs are our theology, and they are a vital part of my life. Running deeper than this, though, is an underground river which comes to the surface, but whether hidden or seen, is the source of true life. This river of life is in every created being, and owes its existence to God, the Creator of all life. Tapping into this river in myself and discovering it in others is the source of my spirituality for the inner city.

---

**Jan Royan is a Roman Catholic who has lived in inner city Sheffield since 1990. She came to do the Study Year at the Urban Theology Unit, where she now tutors part-time – a story told in Gospel From the City.**

What follows are some of the people, events, stories and thoughts that have helped resource my spirituality over the last nine years.

**1. Don't Fence Me In!**

One of the greatest privileges of moving from the Lake District to inner city Sheffield has been living alongside people of other faiths and of other Christian denominations. A short walk from the Roman Catholic presbytery where I live takes me to an Anglican/Methodist church, a Sikh temple, an Anglican church, a URC church, a Methodist church, a Methodist/Baptist/ Ecumenical ex-pub church, a 7th Day Adventist church, a Hindu temple, a Mosque and my own RC church. With two exceptions, I have been able to join in worship in all of these places and have valued that experience.

But God is found not only in places of worship, but in shops, pubs, schools and on the streets. And it is as much in these meetings that I find the God of all life. One of the encounters I most treasure is watching a local Muslim café owner quietly and unobtrusively going down on his knees for evening worship in an unlit part of his café. It is this same man who gives up his time to come to UTU to talk about Islam to a group of students. And who, incidentally, sells the best and cheapest Kashmiri food in Sheffield!

God is big – bigger than we could possibly imagine. Are we trying to control and limit God when we restrict God to only one faith and only one denomination? Thank God for inner cities where the God of life broadens and deepens the river of life within me by these daily encounters with those Christians of other denominations and those of other faiths.

**2. Mutuality of Evangelism**

It took several months before I became aware that I had come to live in an inner city with a colonialist attitude: I had come to "help the poor". And it was several years before the same penny dropped for me at Burngreave Monday Lunch Club. At the end of 1991, a Methodist friend and myself became co-ordinators of Monday Lunch Club for people with learning disabilities. It took a long time for me to realise that I need our people at Monday Lunch Club to break down in me the desire to control and dominate, or to be the one who makes the choices or decisions, and to recognise that they, like God, give me unconditional love, whereas mine is partial. Jon

Sobrino writes that it is the oppressed who show us what it means to be human[1]. Our Lunch Club members, although not generally economically oppressed, suffer oppression because of their lack of choice and because often they are treated as objects rather than subjects of their own lives. And they continually show me the way to be human. One of the volunteers at the club wrote:

> "I needed the company of people other than family and close friends. The opportunity arose in the form of the Lunch Club. I needed to give of myself, but I found I was being taught a lesson in generosity and uncomplicated love and affection, with laughter and happiness that bubbles spontaneously and which I personally needed."

**3. We Cannot Do Everything**

A meditation by Oscar Romero – too long to be quoted in full – throws light on this:

> "We cannot do everything, and there is a sense of liberation in realising that. This enables us to do something, and to do it very well. It may be incomplete, but it is a beginning, a step along the way, an opportunity for the Lord's grace to enter and do the rest." [2]

The river of life in me and the river of life in you need to join so that together we can do something. But in the end we are finite, and it is up to God to continue the work in and through others.

Because we cannot do everything, we must therefore make choices. And it is perhaps as much in the choosing as in the doing that I feel in touch with my own spirituality. If what I most deeply and authentically want is also what God wants for me, then in order to choose I have to peel off the layers of superficiality to find the true desire.

In Nicaragua I touched that spring of authentic desire when I held the hand of a tiny, wrinkled Nicaraguan woman grieving for her husband and sons killed in the Revolution. Afterwards she invited me to her home and to meet her friends. Writing in my diary of that encounter, I said: "At the end I know that this was why I was in Nicaragua – to feel with the women part of the pain and joy of their struggle in the ongoing Revolution."

On my own I could do little to combat the oppression and injustice they suffered, but through a simple touch they allowed me to be in solidarity with them, their strength and their struggle.

## 4. Perseverance

The older I grow the more I admire the resolution and capacity to endure that my mother showed. This was no grim stoicism, but a determination, when she could no longer do something she enjoyed, to find something else which gave her pleasure. Among the people I live with, most of whom have little in terms of worldly goods, I often see this perseverance, this determination to wrest something out of life – even if it's only a win at bingo!

It says to me something about pitting your wits in a virtually non-win situation, of not giving in to the temptation to despair. Often what emerges instead of bitterness, is a wry kind of humour and, in the women in particular, a sharing of the loads they carry.

For anyone who wants to stay the course in inner city ministry, you need your fair share of perseverance, of determination to keep banging on doors – like the importunate widow in Luke's gospel (18: 1-8) – until sometimes the door is opened.

It is that capacity to keep hoping, to keep persevering, to keep praying, and to keep together, which seems to me to be a mark of spirituality in the inner city. It is a grace I often ask for.

## 5. Knowing When To Let Go

It is hard to know sometimes when it is right to let go of a relationship, a job, a struggle, or an attitude of mind. There is a prayer by John V. Taylor which I have often prayed:

> "Father, if the hour has come to make the break, help me not to cling, even though it feels like death. Give me the inward strength of my Redeemer, Jesus Christ, to lay down this bit of life and let it go, so that I and others may be free to take up whatever new and fuller life you have prepared for us, now and hereafter." [3]

We may like Mary Magdalene long to hold the newly risen Christ, but if we want to cling to what is known and safe and reliable, we cannot take the risks necessary for building up God's Kingdom.

A few years ago, some of us in the house tried to build up a relationship with the younger sons of a very difficult family. They came daily to the house, and the only way I found I could continue a relationship with them was by letting go of the awful things they had done the day before, and starting again with them on a new page.

Isn't this what we ask of God when we pray for forgiveness? I think we are asking that our faults and failures of the previous time might be forgiven, so that we can make a new start. We are asking God to let go of our mistakes and to give us another chance.

**6. Vulnerable, but not a Victim**

We have a rule in our house for people who come to the door. We will give food, clothing, talk, occasionally shelter, but not money. That rule is broken all the time! One of the major failings of bureaucracy is that it takes no account of an individual and her/his circumstances. We are often derided for being so foolish (or trusting), but I know that I would rather make the mistake of trusting people, than be eternally suspicious. We are not a bureaucracy, so we can listen to people's stories and requests and make decisions on an individual basis.

Jesus trusted people, and it made him vulnerable. But this was his choice. Better to be vulnerable and to be betrayed, than always to see people as your enemy, constantly to mistrust their motives.

Nevertheless, I see a difference between vulnerability and victimhood. In an inner city you take necessary precautions. You don't invite trouble. But once you've done that, you step out in trust that the God of life will walk with you.

**7. Loving Myself**

If we don't love ourselves, aren't we "spitting in the face of God" as the priest Matthew says in the film 'Priest'? To survive in the city you need to love yourself, and to know when it's right to be gentle with yourself. Otherwise you end up feeling beholden to what a friend of mine describes as a should-y, ought-y God.

We read in the Gospels of Jesus constantly surrounded by people, clamouring for healing and help. Not surprisingly, sometimes he had to get away – to take time out, to be on his own, or with just a few friends.

It's easy to suffer burnout in the inner city, and we have to learn when it's right to say 'no' to the demands made on us, in order to keep going. For myself, my spirituality is bound up with two important considerations:

> - I'm not indispensable. There's a difference between commitment, and the pride of believing that everything will fall to pieces if I'm not there.
> - A discernment between being a helper and being an empowerer. Being a helper allows me to cling to the belief that I'm indispensable; being an empowerer is about allowing people the freedom to do things for themselves.

In the end, I am loving myself when I let go of my desire to be in charge all the time. And it's a real gift to discover that people love me for who I am, not for what I do.

**8. Rooted and Connected**

Like the plants and the trees you see in the city seemingly growing out of brick and concrete and tarmac, I have found nourishment and life from my inner city environment. I have taken root here, I feel at home. I have learnt to find beauty and enjoyment of a different kind.

Next to my house is a Victorian cemetery with magnificent trees, plenty of space and wonderful views of the city. On the rare occasions we have had snow, it is even possible to go sledging there if you watch out for tombstones! I take special pleasure in sniffing the wonderful smells of Asian cooking in the terraced homes nearby. And it is a joy to worship in a church made up of Africans, Anglo-Indians, Anglo-Burmese and people from the Caribbean as well as Irish, Italian, Polish and British people.

**9. Sources, Wells and Places of Refreshment**

For me, one of the difficulties of tapping into the river of life inside me is to do with finding peace and quiet. In a city we are bombarded with sound – traffic, loud music and all the attendant noise of our technological culture. I remember reading about children evacuated to the country during the Second World War who found it frightening either because of the silence or because of the sound of animals. It is machine noise that I generally find distracting and difficult to phase out. Animals, birds, the sound of wind in the trees, or water flowing, are soothing for me, although not for everyone.

Places of comparative tranquillity can be found, even in a busy city. The cemetery is a favourite place, and others have made use of a nearby Anglican retreat house with its chapel on the top floor with enchanting views over the city. Most of the places where I worship offer times of silence within the worship. And, in Sheffield, we are not far from Derbyshire and its beautiful countryside.

Every year there is a possibility of going off for a day's silent retreat within easy driving distance of Sheffield. Lately, these days away have been ecumenical and have been led by a variety of different people. They offer a short input by someone and then one or two hours' time of silent reflection on a Bible passage. These days are important to me because they give time, space and a focus for reflecting on my own vocation in the inner city.

Perhaps the greatest source of refreshment for me has been the discovery of the Ignatian Retreat in Daily Life. This has been developed for people who seek to discover more about their own spirituality, but who have neither the time nor the money to go away for a month. You meet weekly with a Spiritual Director or Accompanier, either singly or in small groups, and share in silence and through the spoken word, your own experiences and feelings of daily directed prayer and Bible readings.

A couple of years ago, doing the Ignatian Retreat in Daily Life, I had a powerful experience of looking into the heart of God. Reflected back to me was an image of what God called me to be – a fully human Jan. And when I looked again, I saw other people, but with a kind of God's-eye view. They, too, became the people God was calling them to be – fully human in their own ways.

It is this image that speaks to me of a God who connects to God's creation through the river of life, forever calling us onward to grow and to become all that we were made to be.

---

1. Jon Sobrino, qtd. C Rowland & M Corner, eds., **Liberating Exegesis**, (SPCK, 1989), p. 49
2. Oscar Romero - Quoted in **Redemptorist Bulletin**, 20 Sept 1998
3. John V Taylor, **A Matter of Life and Death**, SCM Press 1996, p. 67

# Grace Vincent

# WORSHIP AT GRIMESTHORPE

## 1. Sunday Morning: the Event

It's a small room, in fact the little 'front room' of the converted terraced house, which had been a shop and is now our church. A window looks out onto the pavement just outside. Often local children, in curiousity, peer in.

It is 10.15 on a Sunday morning and we are gathering for worship, chatting, asking after each other, laughing with the children. Wilma and Sheila have walked down the road, as has Sarah, hobbling with her stick. Jonathan and Susannah arrive, having walked for half an hour from Pitsmoor pushing the buggy with their two boys. The preacher is here, often the minister, Christine Jones, consulting about songs and hymns. Colin and I arrive with our car loads of five older folk. Susannah bustles around organising the 'big' room for her Sunday School activity. Jenny appears, breathless from some encounter in the road.

Three possible pianists out of a dozen members mean that music is easy, and we all sing lustily, using the old Methodist Hymn Book, UTU's *Hymns of the City*, Galliard's *New Orbit*, or current song sheets.

The children, ages 4 to 13, numbering anything from 3 to 15, sit on the carpet in the middle. The rest of us are on chairs in a circle round the walls.

---

**Grace Vincent has been since 1982 a member, and was for twelve years local Pastor of the Methodist "Corner Shop" at Grimesthorpe in Sheffield's East End, part of the Sheffield Inner City Ecumenical Mission.**

After the first hymn or song, and a prayer, both geared to the kids, we share what the children will do. One of them takes the collection, and they leave with Susannah.

The Bible readings follow, always read round the room, a verse each. People delight to have their turn, often struggling with their eyesight or with difficult words. If something strikes someone in the reading, they easily comment on it.

After more singing, we are at prayer in intercession. In this, we talk together about whatever is concerning us, with names of absent members, or sick friends, neighbours or relatives. The group especially bears a real sense of burden for the troubles of the world. Last Sunday we talked together for at least 10 minutes in anguish about Kosovo and the bombing by Nato. Then the preacher closes with a prayer of 2 or 3 sentences, and we say the Lord's Prayer at this point. The topics people have named do not need to be forced into a final prayer. Our sharing has been the prayer, our caring has been the offering to God.

Then the sermon, which almost always opens out into conversation and reflection. No-one is too shy to have their say. Visiting preachers are advised to makes their initial points important, in case the congregation picks up on them, and they never reach their later points!

After the last singing, the children burst in again and dance around showing us what they have been doing. Or we all have to go into the big room to see their efforts on the walls. Sharona is allowed a few minutes on the piano, learning some hymn tune with one finger. Tea, juice and biscuits appear for all, and we move around chatting, reluctant to break it up and go home.

## 2. A "Fellowship Service" at Grimesthorpe

From time to time we have a Fellowship Service for which everyone is invited to bring a contribution. This can be a favourite hymn, a Bible reading, a poem or reading of any kind. On Sunday 18th April 1999, we had a Fellowship Service. This is what happened when nine of us were present.

We sang 'Lord of the dance' while the children were with us, pointing out that this is not a 'happy, happy' hymn, but one about the dance 'when the sky turns black', too! We had a short prayer and the collection, and the nine children left with Susannah and Colin.

Then it was time to assemble the service. I noted what sorts of contributions each person had brought and put them quickly into some order. We chose two more hymns together – all were from *Hymns of the City* – and then started. This preliminary sharing of what we had each brought was part of the event, too. Interestingly, all three hymns chosen were about the city, its joys and woes – Jesus Christ is waiting (John Bell and Graham Maule), Lord of our city, we bring you its pain (Jane Galbraith), and On the streets of every city, let the love of Christ be seen (David Hill).

Goeff had a moving poem about a derelict old beggar, and one by Wordsworth. Evelyn had been very upset because she had forgotten to bring the poem she had been saving up for the service. Miraculously, Muriel had a copy of it in her bag, as Evelyn had made copies for people at the Lunch Club. So she was jubilant, and read her moving poem about living alone, followed by another, pleading with God to let the writer live till she was 90, which made us all laugh a lot.

Jenny and Jonathan had both independently brought the reading from Luke 24 about the road to Emmaus. We read it verse by verse, round the room. Then Jenny and Jonathan each shared their feelings about it, and how central the story was for one's Christian life. Others chipped in with reflections, so that was our 'word', taking about fifteen minutes.

Jonathan said this story encapsulated for him the whole essence of Christianity – Jesus walking with depressed people, unrecognising, present when they are unaware, then revealed and recognised in simple action with common bread. That is the good news, he said. Jenny spoke of the vivid sense of reality in the account. She especially referred to the unbelievable immediacy of the story, and its affirmation of the presence of Christ in our ordinary lives. Once Jesus was recognised, everything became changed, and they charged back to Jerusalem, completely different people.

Then it was time for intercession. We had a time of silence, thinking about Kosovo, which was so powerfully on everyone's mind, and then another time of silence for Willie, Jenny's son who had just received a very ominous prognosis on the return of a brain cancer. Others then asked prayers for other folk, and we thought about the peace process in Ireland, closing with the Lord's Prayer.

Then came the final hymn and the teas and coffees.

We find an occasional service done this way is tremendously affirming and inclusive. Everyone has a chance to share a treasure, and help create the worship. Folk put aside something lovely or moving or powerful they come across, and save it up for this event. Each of us 'owns' the hour together and has a real part in it. It is a real liturgy – "the people's work".

## 3. Grimesthorpe: the Context

Grimesthorpe Methodist Church "Centre" is two corner shops in the middle of a 1900's neighbourhood of terraced houses. The housing is of the "four houses and a yard" variety, with a "ginnel" between the middle two houses, with a shared yard, and 4 outside toilets. Our shops back on to a single yard. We have replaced the outside toilets with one toilet built on to the corner shop. There is a single room in the corner shop, still with shop windows, which is large enough for a table tennis table or for square tables to seat 20 at the lunch club. Off this leads a smaller "front room" which we call the Chapel ,which has our old communion furniture, a piano, and sixteen chairs around the walls. More chairs are brought in if needed. Behind this room, leading off the larger room, is the kitchen. Upstairs is a flat to house 2 or 3 volunteers or residents.

We opened the "Shop Centre" on 15 June 1980. The original "Statement of Aims" stated that the purpose of the Shop Centre was:

> 1. To provide self-contained accommodation for two to three mission workers.
> 2. To provide small premises for weekday and Sunday church activities and services.
> 3. To provide a shop, store, community facility, craft centre an/or coffee bar, to give the Mission a shop-window and a meeting point with local people.

We elaborated this as:

> Our idea was to create a street-level place of meeting, where various services to the community could exist side by side with an explicitly Christian community, doing its own thing and creating a new generation of disciples. (*Into the City* p.101)

Since 1980, over the years, around twenty people in their twenties have come and lived in the flat and worked with us, usually joining the congregation.

My own association with Grimesthorpe began in 1972. Grimesthorpe Wesley Hall was a 500 – seat "mission hall" in the midst of this depressed post-industrial village. There were 14 members, and I felt I ought to throw in my lot with them. We ran a Friday evening "Sunday School", and kept going in the old building as long as we could. From 1980, when we moved to the shop, we developed a strong participatory worship, for some years with a tea break half way through. From 1985 to 1989, John was the only ordained minister in the Mission, and Local Pastors were appointed in most of the six churches. I was the Local Pastor at Grimesthorpe.

The congregation originally consisted of the older members of the Wesley Hall, the previous building. The last of them died in 1992. We are now a congregation of varied backgrounds, several of them living walking distance from the church. Denominationally, the 13 members are Methodist, Anglican, Baptist, Scottish Presbyterian and Unitarian, but all now count themselves Methodist "members". The area is a mix of young families with children, old people, middle aged, mainly white working class, with some Pakistani families.

The worship service at Grimesthorpe has always been marked by sincerity and significance. In John's book, *Into the City,* he describes the "crucifixion" we experienced in September 1978, when National Front slogans were daubed all over our old chapel, which was being used jointly by the Afro-Caribbean congregation of the New Testament Church of God. In the midst of the trauma of this affront, we held a public occasion, and invited the press. John Greaves was the Church Steward in his eighties:

> A BBC cameramen for Nationwide took pictures and interviewed John Greaves. "If you could get hold of the people who have done this, what would you do?"
>
> Tears rolled down John's cheeks. He bit his lip. Then he said, "If only the people what done this would" – he paused to get the words right – "come to a service, and see the kind of people they have done this to ..."

John continues in his book:

> "What would you say if you were in that situation? If you had a sentence to say to the nation? Would it be that the tiny group of white survivors saying their prayers, or the little black children singing their choruses, would be able to convert the

> powers of evil? That the blood of uncomely saints could be for the conversion of sinners? That strength was in weakness, power in powerlessness – and that the sin of the strong was only in not being prepared to be exposed to the redeeming weakness of the weak?" (*Into the City*, p 99)

## 3. Worship: The People's Work

*The Cities* Report's recommendations include this point:

> City churches are providing Christians everywhere with opportunities for new forms of devotion and prayer, worship, hymnody and meditation. Churches should encourage, and provide support for, such expressions of indigenous and rooted spirituality from and for the city (p. 225).

Grimesthorpe is, I think, a good example of this.

It seems to me that there are three significant and essential characteristics of this kind of worship. First, the room and the numbers are both small. In what larger churches would old or shy and inarticulate people feel free to contribute? Because we know each other well, there is no artificial, formal talk. Conversation is real and about real things, and rarely in "religious" language. Secondly, there is a basic assumption that we are all in this together, that everyone is valued and takes responsibility for what happens. So their thoughts are heard. It is a corporate ministry of all the members. Thirdly, the understanding is that we are there for each other, for the children, for the local community, and for the whole world. The context is tiny, but the brief is vast.

We almost invariably go home stronger and affirmed in our faith, not because we have heard a good sermon (which we certainly often do!), but because the disciples of Jesus have been building each other up for our work in the world.

---

Books referred to:
**Hymns of the City**, ed. John Vincent. Urban Theology Unit, Rev. Ed. 1998
**New Orbit**, ed. Peter Smith. Galliard, Rev. Ed. 1984
John Vincent, **Into the City**, Epworth Press. 1982
**The Cities: A Methodist Report**, NCH Action for Children, 1997

Mike Simpson
and Joan Sharples

# CONSULTATION AND CELEBRATION

## 1. The Background.

A series of British Liberation Theology Consultation and Celebration Weekends has taken place at two year intervals since an initial gathering at Upholland College, near Wigan, in 1989. Subsequent weekends have been held at Wistaston Hall, a retreat and conference centre near Crewe run by a Catholic religious order, the Oblates, and organised by Mike Simpson and Joan Sharples of Las Casas with the assistance of an advisory team. The somewhat ponderous title, while necessary to define the nature of these meetings, was inevitably shortened to BLT. Although Mike was present at the first Consultation, he was not a member of the planning group and we have been reliant on the notes and recollections of some who were, in preparing an account of the origins of the project.

The consultations originated in a conversation between John Vincent of the Urban Theology Unit in Sheffield and Chris Rowland, then of Cambridge University, who was conducting a seminar on liberation theology at UTU in

---

**Mike Simpson: Former Justice and Peace Fieldworker for the Diocese of Shrewsbury. Secretary of Las Casas Network, co-ordinator of the information network "Colombia Forum", and organiser of BLTCC weekends.**
**Joan Sharples: Current Justice and Peace Fieldworker for the Diocese of Shrewsbury and co-worker with Mike Simpson in Las Casas & BLTCC.**

the spring of 1988. Since his return from a first visit to Brazil in 1983, Chris had been very conscious that while there were many examples of individuals or groups engaged in the praxis of liberation theology in Britain, they were frequently operating in isolation and often without knowledge of one another. This was in striking contrast to the far more organised and inter-related context which he had encountered in Latin America. Chris and John agreed on the need for an ecumenical networking initiative which could bring such people together, and prepared a joint letter of invitation to a planning meeting which was sent to a large number of people working in the field. The meeting was held on 4 July 1988 at UTU, those present being: Terry Drummond, Laurie Green, Margaret Hebblethwaite, Marie Howes, Bridget Rees, John Rogerson, Chris Rowland, Hilary Russell, Peter Scott, David Skidmore, John Vincent, and Haddon Wilmer.

The issues raised at this initial meeting are worth recording, for they were to exercise the minds of the Consultation organisers in years to come. A sharing of responses to the concept of a Consultation raised a number of points: that liberation theology offered hope for renewal to a church in decline; that it could be a way of offering theological reflection on individual and communal stories; that the insights of the Christian Base Communities might be a resource for a contemporary political spirituality; that an exchange of experience would be valuable; and that the methodology of liberation theology was a way forward to empower ordinary people. At the same time it was recognised that there were tensions involved in doing this theology in the context of the institutional church.

The subsequent discussion revealed some of the anomalies and tensions which were to be a feature of the Consultations. The group was conscious of being one made up of white middle-class "professionals"; in particular the absence of blacks, who made up a significant proportion of the marginalised community, was noted. Was the event aimed at "armchair theologians of liberation" or at people from the grassroots? Was it to be one which would be a means of "conscientising the comfortable" or one which recognised itself to be peripheral in the life of the churches? And what was it for? There was general agreement that a main aim was to make it a "confidence-building exercise of sharing with other practitioners". Listening to people's stories and exchanging and learning from experiences should play a vital part, though some felt that "the practitioners need to move to theological reflection as well as just story-telling". It was felt that the Consultation should offer some degree of "training" so that those at the grassroots could "theologise and reflect in ways they thought they could not manage". The tool of the pastoral cycle (or spiral) with its sequence of the exploration of communal experience (or reality), social analysis, theological reflection, and action and finally celebration was suggested as a means to this end.

There was a strong feeling that the event should not exist in a contextual vacuum, but should relate to the specific state of political and ecclesiastical life in the country. At the same time there was a consciousness of the danger of feeling that by merely setting it up the organisers would have done something when the "left" was in the grip of a political malaise. There was a need to struggle with imperfections of the world and not resort to naive optimism. Above all, it had to be recognised that the Consultation was not a definitive event offering an answer.

By the end of the day, it had been determined that the aim of the Consultation was to provide an opportunity for a celebration of the emergence of British practitioners of liberation theology and a platform for participants to be heard and offer and receive support. The format adopted should not be didactic, but should arise from the experience of the participants, who should ideally number about fifty and meet at some venue north of Watford. The participation was to be made up of practitioners of liberation theology and those who lived and worked at the grass roots out of a liberationist perspective. A planning group for the first Consultation was set up, with people of different backgrounds and working in a variety of contexts: Terry Drummond, Marie Howes, Bridget Rees, Chris Rowland, David Skidmore.

## 2. The First Consultation, 1989

In exploring the background to the First Consultation, we have nothing but admiration for the work of the planning group who clearly worked extremely hard at what must have been a very difficult task. Its members did not know one another well, came from different parts of the country, and worked in different contexts – though this, of course, was valuable in terms of publicising the event. The group was also handicapped by the inability of John Vincent to be part of the planning group, as between June 1989 and June 1990 he was doing his full-time year as President of the Methodist Conference. However, while it was autonomous, there existed in the minds of its members a sense that John's surmised views needed to be taken into account, both because he had been joint convenor of the original meeting and because as Director of the Urban Theology Unit with a lifetime's experience in that field, his perspective was of great importance. On the other hand, his physical absence in the deliberations of the planning group left him, like Banquo's ghost, a kind of spectral presence whose ideas might be anticipated but not debated with him.

The wide publicity given to the event produced a large number of enquiries and applications. The policy of restricting participation to practitioners of liberation theology in the British context meant that those wishing to attend were required to furnish an account of their involvement. With the demand for places exceeding supply in any case, it was necessary to refuse admission to those not possessing the appropriate wedding garment. Attention was also paid to the geographical distribution of participants, to securing a balance of men and women, and to ensuring black participation.

The venue settled upon, many other enquiries having proved unfruitful, was Upholland College, near Wigan, a former Catholic seminary, built in the last century to mass-produce priests to service the religious needs of the burgeoning Irish diaspora. Its massive size, vast corridors and lofty rooms, the sheer weight of stone confidently asserting that the Catholic church was back to reconquer England for the Faith, made it a curious context for an ecumenical meeting of those doing theology on the margins of, or outside the churches, though its present emptiness provided an interesting objective correlative of the crisis confronting those institutions. Perhaps those who regarded liberation theology as a vital agent in church renewal might have derived some comfort from the fact that possibly some seeds of a new creation were being sown in these surroundings in the course of this meeting, thought it seems to us that this is to put the cart before the horse: the church exists to serve the world, not the praxis of justice to serve the church.

The programme was designed to ensure a maximum degree of sharing of experience in small groups, with plenary input being restricted to three short "story-telling" sessions on the Saturday morning and a presentation on work in Liverpool by Neville Black during the evening of that day. Saturday afternoon was taken up with an "exposure" visit to a project in Skelmersdale, a nearby Liverpool overspill town hard-hit by the Thatcher years.

The Consultation proved of great value in bringing together people from across the denominations, many previously unknown to one another but working in similar or related fields, and the emphasis on the sharing of stories and experience at the heart of it has remained fundamental in subsequent Consultations. It was anything but a cosy get-together of people of like mind, however, revealing problems and tensions which created difficulties for the organising team and remained unresolved in the course of the weekend.

Part of the difficulty was implicit in the title, which suggested the existence of one body of thought which could correctly be defined as liberation theology. Consciously, or unconsciously, this was being identified with the work done and the religious insights articulated out of the context of the urban marginalised and dispossessed. There was no overt recognition that there is no liberation theology as such, but only liberation theologies emerging from the experience of the oppressed in their struggles – whether these were women, or blacks, or people working in the field of ecology – some of whom, particularly in the first category, felt resentment that their agendas had not received sufficient attention. There was tension also between those who rightly pointed out that all liberation theology is contextual and asserted that therefore the British version had nothing to learn from the experience of those in the South, and others who felt that such experience was valuable. Even amongst the "urban theologists" there were differences of opinion about how it should be done – orthodoxy, in this field as in others, is *my* doxy! There was criticism too of the make-up of the Consultation. The great majority of participants were either clergy or lay people working in official church agencies, and those who were themselves the objects rather than the subjects of economic history were noticeable only by their absence.

It might be concluded from this description that the event was something of a disaster, which is far from being the case. The conflicts and tensions in fact were an inevitable part of bringing together deeply committed people involved in a variety of struggles ("wounded practitioners" as John Vincent later described them) with their own particular sensitivities. The painful dialectic, though remaining unresolved, was perhaps a necessary part of the process of finding new ways of being Church in the world.

Nevertheless, for the organising team the event had proved a fraught experience, with differences of opinion arising amongst its members in the course of the weekend. The situation was not improved in the final plenary session when one participant accused them of promoting a hidden and self-interested agenda. There was too little recognition in this uncomfortable session of the hard work and dedication which had gone into this breaking of new ground. It was hardly surprising that when the question of a future Consultation was raised, the team refused to have any part in its implementation. The value of their initiative was, however, apparent in the strong feeling amongst many participants that the event should be repeated.

Mike was amongst those who felt that the event had been a valuable one and should continue. With a reckless disregard of what he was letting Las Casas in for, he indicated his willingness to be part of a team to organise a future event if others present would join him in this. Stanley Baxter, Ed O'Connell, John Vincent and Eileen White agreed to do so, the group later being expanded to include at various times David Cowling, Andrew Deuchar, Ann Gill, Laurie Green, Mary Grey, Betty Luckham, Austin Smith, Liz Stuart, Romy Tiongco and Margaret Walsh. In practice, however, for a variety of reasons, the organisation of future Consultations was to become the responsibility of Las Casas, with the other members giving support and fulfilling a consultancy role. After a brief meeting of some members of the planning team early in 1991, it was agreed that future discussion should be by telephone, with Mike co-ordinating the collective observations of its members.

## 3. Las Casas

Las Casas had originated in the activities of a small Justice and Peace group in the Catholic Parish of St Anne, Nantwich, in 1984, which had opted to focus mainly, though not exclusively, on issues of social justice and human rights in Latin America. In January 1986 it had begun the distribution of the Nicaraguan letters from Fr. John Medcalf, who was working in Muelle de los Bueyes, in the war zone of Zelaya Central. This in turn led to the distribution of those of other socially committed priests and religious working amongst the poor in Venezuela, Peru, Ecuador, El Salavador and Bolivia. By the beginning of 1988, the network included over two hundred individuals, communities, organisations and groups, religious and secular, from a wide variety of contexts in Great Britain and Ireland. Las Casas's access to other sources of information on Latin America not generally available led also to requests for information on a variety of specific subject areas in the Latin American field, and increasingly for material on liberation theologies.

In January 1987 it was decided to adopt the name "Las Casas" for the network – not an acronym, but commemorating the conscientising activities of Bartolome de Las Casas, while also reflecting its liberation-theology dimension. (Las Casas is an exemplar for Christians of the popular church in Latin America, and Gustavo Gutierrez's centre at Rimac is called the Las Casas Centre). In response to a felt need, a centre was developed to make available to the network a wide range of books and other resources on Latin America, on development and the environment, and on liberation, creation and peace theologies. The small profits which accrued helped to defray the costs of a small organisation operating on a shoe-string budget with unpaid full-time workers and no external funding.

By the end of the eighties, Las Casas had built up considerable experience in organising tours for overseas speakers, conferences, theological seminars an days or weekends of reflection. In 1988 it had also become responsible for the organisation of the *December Group* weekend, an institution which reached back to the interface of left wing politics and Christian faith associated with the *Slant* movement in the Catholic church in the early sixties, which centred around Dominican intellectuals in Oxford and elsewhere. The Las Casas involvement resulted in the creation of a new constituency for the December weekend, largely issuing from Justice and Peace and related fields in Britain, with an ambience which was more ecumenical, more related to praxis and less "intellectual" than formerly.

It had also built up a network of committed activists from the radical margins of the churches, religious congregations, justice and peace, human rights and solidarity organisations, and political groups, often working in isolation and alienated from their context. The aim was to inform, support, empower and to bring them together on an organic model rather than in terms of formal structures, providing a service which enabled groups or organisations to fulfil their own agendas. A fundamental principle was never to seek to impose the Las Casas agenda on others, or to convert the network into an organisation with specific membership, since this would ultimately make it an institution more concerned about the continuity of its own existence than its praxis.

In practice, the Las Casas constituency and its work overlap considerable with those of the justice and peace movement in Britain, which, in its more radical manifestations at least, is underpinned by theologies of liberation. Mike in 1988 and later Ann Gill and Joan were employed as (badly!) paid J&P fieldworkers for the diocese of Shrewsbury, Joan becoming the first Anglican fieldworker employed by a Catholic diocese in the country, following a temporary period of employment for Christian Aid. The justice and peace agenda led to a greater emphasis on home-based issues than hitherto, while at the same time expanding the network of contacts.

With access, therefore, to a national network and considerable organising experience we felt confident of our capacity to organise just another weekend every two years. In fact, the Consultation was to be our greatest challenge – and provide our biggest headaches – in the years to come. Organising a Justice and Peace conference for four hundred participants with three or four major speakers, a dozen seminars and even more workshops proved relatively easy in comparison!

**4. The Second Consultation, 1991**

The new organisers were handicapped, of course, in that no members of the original team were willing to participate in the preparation of the next event. Nevertheless, we were determined to learn from the experience of the First Consultation to overcome some of the problems that had arisen. As already indicated, it was felt that the implicit definition of liberation theology had been too narrow, and that while we needed to retain the emphasis on praxis – in other words, it was not to be a conference of academics – participation should be widened. The initial letter of invitation to potential participants made this policy clear:

> This weekend is seen not primarily as a meeting of academics in the field (though we would not wish to exclude any who might wish to attend) but as a conference for practitioners involved in various liberation struggles. It is difficult to produce a definitive list of who these might be, but they might include, e.g. those involved in grassroots activity among the urban poor, in black communities, or in the feminist movement, members of base Christian communities, or those acting in solidarity with the oppressed at home or abroad and sharing their reading of reality and fundamental praxis.

We felt it important to involve all those wishing to attend in the planning process. Accordingly, they were invited in the same letter to indicate their hopes and expectations for the weekend with their replies.

It was also felt necessary to redress an imbalance noted earlier – the preponderance of clergy and lay church employees – to secure the participation of more people living and working at the grassroots and of the marginalised themselves. This meant, of course, keeping the cost of the weekend as low as possible and being prepared to subsidise some of those wishing to attend, if necessary in full. We had the benefit of a small surplus from the First Consultation as a "float", but in the absence of external funding (and we lacked the time and indeed the inclination to tour possible funding organisations with a begging bowl) the resources for this had to be provided for in the charge for the weekend, as well as covering the cost of publicity. This too had to be kept to a minimum. There was no question of expensive press advertisements and we were reliant on the networks available to the organising team and its supporters.

A partial solution to these financial problems lay in the choice of Wistaston Hall as the new venue for the weekend, the charges being little more than half those made by most conference centre. Its location was also important, fairly central in the country, only a mile and half from Crewe, a major railway junction to and from which we could provide a "taxi" service, and within easy reach of the M6. On the other hand, we were not unaware that the comforts and relaxed ambience of a former home of the rural gentry set in pleasant surroundings provided a setting as inappropriate in its own way as had been Upholland.

There were some sixty replies from would-be participants to the initial letter of invitation which was sent out at the beginning of March 1991. It was obvious from the responses to our request for observations on themes to be addressed and perceived agendas that we would have our work cut out to satisfy the diversity of interests indicated within the time-span of a weekend. Themes suggested included an exploration of "the state of play". What was the current situation in post-colonial, post-industrial, post-Thatcher Britain? What were the likely repercussions of the post-socialist new Europe? How were we to confront the structures of oppression rather than ameliorate their consequences? How were we to do a liberation theology in the context of a largely middle-class, affluent society and a male-dominated hierarchic and conservative church? What was the role of liberation theology in the decade of evangelism? Had we anything to learn from the reflection and praxis of those in the South?

The particular agendas of potential participants exhibited a considerable diversity. Many were working in areas of urban deprivation, either within established church structures or by living out alternative ways of being church. Others were operating within the context of a theology of solidarity with the South. Some were articulating the black experience and struggle, and others were engaged in interfaith or intercultural dialogue. Many of the women were committed to the feminist agenda. A feeling was also present that the issue of marginalistion as a consequence of people's sexuality as well as their sex needed to be addressed. Some interest was expressed in exploring the interface between liberation, peace and creation theologies.

In terms of the structure of the weekend, people's ideas were rather more vague, but there was clearly some desire for a degree of plenary input, for the exploration of methodologies and skills associated with liberation theology – e.g. the use of the pastoral cycle/spiral, the use of social analysis as a tool, the creation of first-world base communities – and for the communication of experience by storytelling. For others, the opportunity to meet and share was felt to be the principal object of the weekend.

Having found, we trusted, what people wanted, we were faced with the problem of responding to the heterogeneous nature of the ideas which had been presented to us in creating some structure through which these could be addressed. The information we received was collated and sent with details of those interested in attending to other members of the organising group, and a meeting was held in May for those who were able to attend at Upholland, where several had been taking part in a conference. Constraints of time meant that detailed discussion proved impossible, and it was agreed that we should be responsible for the organisation of the weekend and confer with the other members by telephone. Certain ideas did emerge, however, which we attempted to put into practice in structuring the event.

One was the creation of affinity groups bringing together people of similar or related agendas for experience-sharing, an idea which was implemented in the Second and Third Consultations. Another was the formation of a group of "Listeners" who would attempt to tune in to the feelings and opinions of participants regarding the strengths and weaknesses of the structure and organisation of the weekend, and to report back through a spokesperson in the final plenary session – a process which, it was felt, would save time and be valuable for the organisation of any future Consultation. In the event, this proved to be unsuccessful, as the group itself failed to arrive at any consensus which could be presented, and the idea was subsequently abandoned. There was also to be a Liturgy Group to plan a Celebration for the Saturday evening with each affinity group contributing something of the fruit of their deliberations, and a short closing liturgy before lunch on Sunday. There was also to be a communion service on Saturday and a Catholic Mass on Sunday before breakfast with all welcome to participate. We were conscious that a number of people might be grateful for an opportunity to promote the cause of particular organisations or sell resources, and so provided a "market place" session in which stalls/exhibitions could be manned in the main hall within the context of a period of general socialising.

There were over seventy registrations for this Consultation, and though inevitably there were some last minute cancellations as a result of illness or other domestic crises, sixty five attended – a number which was to present us with some logistical problems within the constraints of the space and number of rooms available in the building, though these were coped with reasonably well. Participants had been asked to join particular affinity groups along the lines of their personal agendas as indicated above, two of these being subdivided in the event because they proved too large to be viable within the consultative framework. The affinity groups were on Marginalisation, Racial Issues, Third World Solidarity, Confronting Powers, and Poverty and Deprivation. Participants were also required to choose various story-telling groups and issue groups, so that they would, it was hoped, be able to bring back a variety of experience to their affinity groups. Details of the membership of these groups, together with a list of participants with brief biographical information was sent out shortly before the event.

The story-telling groups provided an opportunity to listen to people chosen from the participants themselves who, we believed, had particularly interesting stories to tell. There would be an opportunity for questions and discussion and for a sharing of group members' personal experience in relation to the story-teller's narrative. The first story-telling group was led by Breda Noonan, a Columban sister whose twenty three years in the Philippines in the service of the poor represented both a personal faith journey and a paradigm of the radical church's progress from welfare activity to the empowerment and accompanying of grassroots communities. She now lived in Birmingham, giving training in community-building techniques to Columban postulants, working in inter-faith relations in her own multi-ethnic areas of the city, and studying group therapy. The second group was led by Sylvia Sands, who had worked in Ireland as a peacemaker, initially amongst the Tartan gangs of the Shankhill, and later on both sides of the sectarian divide. For some years she had run an ecumenical peace-retreat centre in Donegal, based on Franciscan spirituality. She was now, once again, in Belfast working (full time but unpaid) with a variety of marginalised groups in the city – the homeless, the gay community, aids sufferers and ex-prisoners – in the Oasis Trust which she had founded. The third story-teller was Austin Smith, a Passionist priest who for the previous twenty years lived and worked among the inner city community of Liverpool 8 (Toxteth) and for some years acted as prison chaplain in the city. His work was to try "to understand and critique the situation of the powerless from the philosophical and theological standpoint ... to help church and society recognise the sinfulness of that situation and to place it on their agendas, not as a marginal ameliorating activity, but in the perceiving of the fact that human liberation and control of one's destiny is a central part of the development of the Kingdom of God" – an ongoing process of reflection which he has shared with those he has accompanied in their struggle to achieve human dignity. In the fourth group, Liz Stuart and Jane Robson told their story of an attempt to bring Gay Liberation to the church and Christ to the lesbian and gay community. The fifth story was that of the Hope Community, which since 1985 had provided a religious/lay Christian presence in Heath Town, Wolverhampton, a high-rise and semi-high rise estate built some twenty years ago and characterised by high unemployment and poverty, racial tensions and problems with drug-trafficking and prostitution. The aim has been "to accompany people … being and building community". Margaret Walsh, who had been part of the project since it began, told its story with the help of others from Heath Town.

The issue groups were established to cover various topics in which a number of people had expressed an interest and felt needed to be addressed during the weekend. We had identified participants with a particular expertise in these fields to lead the groups from amongst those attending. The topics included *Methodology for Groups: Simple Tools for Social Analysis and the Action Theology Spiral* (Laurie Green); *Models for British Base Christian Communities* (Margaret Hebblethwaite); *Liberation Theology and the Decade of Evangelism* (Simon Barrow); *The Churches and Homelessness: Amelioration or Confronting the Causes?* (Chris Allen); *Liberation Theology and Inter-faith* Dialogue (David Herbert).

Plenary input was restricted to a seventy-minute session on Friday evening and one of similar length on Saturday morning. On Friday, Bishop Patrick Kalilombe of the Centre for Black and White Christian Partnership welcomed the participants and Chris Rowland presented *The Challenge of the Nineties for Liberation Theology*. This was followed by short interventions by Myra Poole, representing a feminist viewpoint, and Janet Hodgson who spoke on the importance of recognising the global aspect of the struggle. A period of open discussion followed. In a fifty-minute session on Saturday morning, Ian Fraser did a short presentation, Slings and Pebbles: Theological Tools for Confrontation, and John Vincent summed up the emerging themes and agendas. Affinity group sessions followed[1], with the story-telling groups meeting in the afternoon and the issue groups on Sunday morning. Saturday evening was taken up with a lively liturgical celebration.

The final plenary session before lunch on the Sunday (together with subsequent correspondence) provided some insight into the success of the weekend. We had, of course, been aware of inevitable tensions inherent in mixing people from so many perspectives and once again there was a feeling amongst many of the women present that the feminist viewpoint was not sufficiently appreciated by the men. There was clearly a sharp division of opinion between those who wanted more input and direction, and those who gained most from being with and sharing with others engaged in a common mission. The attempt to resolve these two points of view, of satisfying the needs of what we irreverently came to refer to as the Anarchists and the

Stalinists was to remain a problem. Though criticisms were voiced and doubtless more remained unvoiced in this final session, there was a general feeling that the Consultations should continue and that Las Casas should be responsible for the organisation.

## 5. The Third Consultation, 1993

In order to prepare for the Third Consultation, we again asked prospective participants for their suggestions regarding the issues they wished to see addressed in the course of the weekend. Suggestions on themes indicated that participants were conscious of a need to reassess the current situation nationally and globally – "to read the signs of the times" – in the light of developments over the previous two years. There was a feeling that we must share the problems of organising for change in both society and church, to explore and analyse ways of building and empowering communities, and to strengthen links between all grassroots movements, developing a global agenda. The alarming rise of fascism and racism in Europe as a whole was also a subject of concern.

In this context we needed to consider, in global terms, the collapse of the traditional socialist models of Eastern Europe; the triumphalism associated with the apparent victory of neo-liberal economics and the philosophy (and theology) associated with it; the decline of development capitalism and its substitution by a "wild cat" model far more destructive of communities and environments, in which large sections of the world's population were simply superfluous to the economic process – and essentially, therefore, non-people; paradoxically, the *crisis* of international capitalism ensuing from the end of the Cold War and the break up of the Soviet bloc; the resurgence of racism, nationalism, and fascism and the Fortress Europe – and Fortress Britain – mentality. Plus, more and more marginalised people were living on shrinking hand-outs and were perceived as having no real stake in society.

In the context of all this, Latin American theologian Pablo Richard had recently argued in an article that liberation theology must enter a new phase[2]. Hitherto, it had operated in a critical role similar to that of the early prophets, whose utterances were made in the context of a traditional social order and accepted social norms, however corrupt and unjust the powerful elites in that society had become. Now he suggested the context had changed: we were captives in Babylon and what we needed to develop was an apocalyptic theology, a theology of vision and hope to sustain the people of God in a dark time.

In the light of this scenario and the concerns and themes suggested by intending participants, we asked affinity groups to reflect upon these things in relation to their particular contexts and to share their reflections at a plenary level. There would be an opportunity to listen to people's stories and share participants' own experience in story-telling groups. It was hoped that the Consultation might begin to address a number of questions:

a) What seeds of hope could be perceived in the present situation?
b) Was there a need for a new "apocalyptic" theology, and if so, how could this be formulated?
c) Given shrinking state and local government provision, how could we develop broad-based community programmes which were empowering and met people's real needs, but which were not susceptible to manipulation or hi-jacking?
d) How could change be brought about in a generally conservative, hierarchical, patriarchal, and theologically disconnected church, which could itself be oppressive and part of the problem?
e) How could we take on a global agenda which recognised the importance and validity of all liberation struggles and sought to bring together all of them in a consensus of resistance to the present order of things?

In the light of the suggested themes for the weekend outlined above, we asked Ian Linden of the Catholic Institute for International Relations to present an overview, *Objectively Disordered: The Global Economy,* in the opening plenary session on Friday evening, and this was followed by A *Theological Critique of Neo-liberal Ideology* by John Vincent. The strong interest in ways of building communities reflected in participants' initial replies we sought to answer through a plenary session on Saturday afternoon which provided contrasting approaches. In the first session, Zulia Mena spoke of OBAPO, an umbrella organisation of black communities on Colombia's Pacific Coast involved in the struggle to maintain their environment and traditional way of life in the face of the Colombian government's grandiose economic Plan Pacifico. In the second, Keith Argyle gave an account of the Salford Urban Mission initiative and Gina and Ray McCall described the work in Port Clarence, an "urban village" near Middlesborough with massive unemployment, where community action had achieved remarkable results. The story-telling input, entitled Faith Journeys, was to be supplied by David Cowling and Luis Correa of Grassroots, Ian Fraser, Tracts Harney and Eileen White, though Ian was, in fact, unable to attend at the last moment.

The affinity groups proposed for the weekend on the basis of initial responses encompassed:

1) Those experiencing or working in a context of urban or rural poverty and deprivation, subdivided into a) those who were members of base communities or engaged in building community, b) those working for agencies, c) those working in the institutional church context.
2) Those experiencing, or working in the field of homelessness
3) Those working in solidarity with The South
4) Those operating in the context of marginalisation by society and church on grounds of sex or sexuality
5) Those struggling for racial justice, working with refugees or immigrants or concerned with interfaith issues
6) Those engaged in the struggle for peace and disarmament
7) Those committed to an ecological agenda
8) People struggling for justice for those marginalised in a variety of social contexts: e.g. amongst the elderly, the mentally ill, victims of violence or sexual abuse, those with disabilities, people suffering from AIDs.

To our surprise only two participants, who knew one another very well, elected to be members of the group struggling against the marginalisation of people on grounds of their sex or sexuality. Categories 2, 6, 7 and 8 also failed to elicit viable groups so that the final groups were 1a, 1c, 3 and 5 with a fifth group of people working in a variety of contexts.

With the number of participants on this occasion being smaller than at the Second Consultation, we were presented with fewer logistical problems. It was good too, to have with us more people from the South – from India, West Africa and four from Latin America – though the candid statement from one of them that "you've hardly got started over here" was hardly encouraging for some participants. Some features of the weekend, however, were less than successful. Zulia Mena's input suffered in the absence of the professional interpreter who had accompanied her during her two-week national tour of the country and placed too little emphasis on the development of community structures, so that the hoped-for comparison between North-South community organising did not clearly emerge. More fundamental were problems associated with the affinity groups in certain of which friction was apparent. In particular, the absence of a women's group excited strong criticism – unfairly, we felt, since hitherto no one had indicated that they wanted one. What we had failed to appreciate was a need not so much to address specific women's issues, as to provide a space in which a variety of things could be discussed within a shared consciousness as women. This felt need was met when those concerned transformed Tracts Harney's Faith Journey session into a women's discussion group.

The final plenary session once again revealed the dichotomy between the "Stalinist/Anarchist" approaches to what the Consultation should be about, with some of those present strongly advocating a more structured approach in which a process with a specific end in view was of greater significance than the informal meeting of minds favoured by others, perhaps the majority of participants. There was a feeling among some that we should be working towards the production of some kind of "manifesto" and that the Consultation should provide the basis for a permanent liberation theology think-tank on the model of the South African Institute of Contextual Theology, with the implication that the Consultation organisers should somehow be responsible for this. As far as we were concerned this was simply not an option, for we had neither the financial nor the human resources to pursue such a course of action, however supportive we might be of the idea of bringing to laudable an ambition to fruition. Moreover, it did not seem to be what the initiators of the Consultations had conceived them to be about – and was certainly not what we had "signed up" for as organisers. In fact, the yearly 3-day Institute in Sheffield fulfils some of this aim.

In view of our misgivings concerning the success of the weekend, it was perhaps surprising that there was a strong feeling that the Consultations should continue and that we should organise the 1995 event. We agreed to do so, albeit somewhat reluctantly, in the absence of any expressed willingness on the part of others to assume this responsibility.

## 6. The Fourth Consultation, 1995

As we approached the Fourth Consultation, it seemed to us that in general the analysis of our reality presented for the previous one remained valid. However, the current context appeared to be one which presented a picture of greater confusion, contradiction and paradox than had been the case two years before. One the one hand, the British Government seemed to be pressing ahead with its neo-liberal agenda, despite the fact that the new government line-up was perceived as being further to the left than its predecessor. On the other, the Labour Party seemed prepared to administer a diluted version of the neo-liberal model which excluded large sections of the population from genuine social participation, while at the same time advancing a communitarian ethic which could not but be inimical to the philosophical system lying behind the economic model which, in general, it appeared to be willing to retain.

As on previous occasions, we began our preparations for the Fourth Consultation by asking potential participants to identify their agendas and suggest possible themes. The response produced a bewildering multiplicity of disparate material. This made us reflect more deeply about the nature of the affinity groups, which in the past had been proposed on the basis of some similarity of agenda emerging from initial responses. This time there appeared to be almost as many agendas as participants. Moreover, we felt that the practice of having participants "sign up" in advance for these groups had not proved particularly successful at the previous Consultation and our experience was also that agendas did tend to change, and that people arrived with ideas which they wished urgently to communicate and discuss that might well not have been reflected in their original application forms.

Joan therefore proposed a different process for the weekend. The session on Friday evening was to be largely devoted to a plenary sharing of current concerns, with each participant having a couple of minutes to express them. Out of this listening process, it was hoped, affinities would emerge and coalesce to form the basic groups for the weekend sessions, which would present the fruit of their deliberations in whatever form they wished within a liturgical context in a final plenary session on Sunday morning. Ann Gill, our colleague in our justice and peace work and always our closest collaborator, was also in favour of this approach. Mike was more dubious given the nature of the participation, very much for the idea in theory, but doubtful whether, in practice, those present would be able to reach a consensus about what these groups might be and make personal decisions about which to join, within the constraints of the time period available. Nevertheless, he allowed himself to be persuaded. It was obvious that a skilled facilitator would be necessary for the process, and we called upon Romy Tiongco, who had a wealth of experience in the facilitation of groups both in the Philippines and Britain, to undertake this task. In the event, the participants committed themselves to the process. The knowledge that time was limited concentrated minds and gave urgency to what was said, and the depth of sharing and sensitive listening far beyond a polite exchange of names and job descriptions, carried the process forward far better than even Joan had anticipated.

At the end of the session, Romy tentatively suggested areas of concern and negotiated the formation of groups in dialogue with those present. Interestingly, these were less concerned with particular agendas than with methods of approach. Two groups were dedicated to the exploration of alternative visions to our current reality. The emphasis in the first was on the political and economic alternatives to the neo-liberal model, while the other devoted itself to a critique of neo-liberal ideology and discussion of the articulation of an alternative theological and spiritual vision. The concentration in the third group was on strategies for action, and the fourth a group intended for "women who want to talk about all these issues with other women" (though in fact the group was to be joined by a man). In practice the latter became one of personal sharing, affirmation and empowerment.

It will be seen that in adopting this new approach, we were coming down unambiguously on the side of the "anarchists". The groups were required to own the process and organise themselves through whatever facilitative techniques they chose, a process which some found difficult. For the same reason, formal plenary input was largely eschewed and restricted to a Saturday evening report on the UN Conference on Women at Beijing, from which Marie Power, the speaker, had recently returned.

We retained the story-group sessions, Projects, Issues and Faith Journeys, however, since we felt that in general these had been successful. These occupied two sessions following an initial meeting of affinity groups. In the first, Donald Nicholl, academic, theologian and former Rector of the Ecumenical Institute at Tantur, Jerusalem, reflected on his life, from his working class background in the West Riding to his lifetime involvement in the struggle for peace. Christine Nixon spoke of the work of The Roby, a URC-based open-door community project in inner city Manchester, which she had founded ten years before. Margaret Walsh, who had described the work of the Hope Community in Heath Town, Wolverhampton, at the 1991 Consultation, updated her group on the progress of the Community's work in the four years which had passed since then.[3]

In the second session, Mary Beasley spoke of her work with alcohol and drug abusers which complemented, rather than duplicated, existing services, and her interest in work on the margins as a potential place of renewal for the churches. Abina Parshad-Griffin, a working-class black woman then studying at Westminster College, Oxford told of her personal struggle. David Rhodes, a project worker with Faith in Leeds and head of the One City Project, an experiential learning programme to help suburban churches to respond to issues of social injustice in non-paternalistic ways described the work of the project and also his voluntary work with the homeless and alcoholics. We seized the opportunity to ask Ian Fraser, who had spent fifty years articulating a people's theology and was an international authority on Base Communities, to tell the fourth story – one originally planned for 1993.

As we approached the end of the weekend, we felt that the new approach had been justified. Though inevitably there had been tensions and dissatisfactions – especially over an impromptu digression by a small group on the Saturday evening which interfered with the timetable and was resented by some – the Consultation had been less conflictive than on early occasions. There was, however, some cause for concern with regard to the participation which seemed less representative geographically and denominationally than formerly, with the majority of participants coming from the North West or the Midlands and half of them being Catholics. This did not seem of paramount importance, however, since Joan was firmly of the opinion that this should be the last Consultation that we should organise.

The future of the Consultation therefore very much exercised the minds of participants in the final plenary session and discussion on this subject went on for some time, incidentally squeezing out a final reflection by Austin Smith, which had been an enriching experience on previous occasions. Despite some criticisms, it became apparent that the general feeling was that the Consultations were of value and must continue – and that it was up to Las Casas to organise them, since no one else felt able to undertake the task. We were moved by the expressions of trust placed in us, not only by those whom we had known for years, but also by people we had met for the first time, and since our raison d'etre has always been one of service, we felt it impossible not to yield to the pressure to organise the Fifth Consultation.

## 7. The Fifth Consultation, 1997

The 1997 meeting proved to be different from earlier Consultations in a number of ways. The most obvious of these was that there were fewer participants. In part this could be explained by a clash of dates. Official duties meant that a number of people who had been present at earlier weekends were unable to attend this one. Even allowing for this, however, the number of registrations was low, just under thirty rather than around fifty.

Though the smaller number meant that our task as organisers was made easier in that there were fewer logistical problems, it raised a number of significant questions for us. Was the concept of the Wistaston Hall Consultation an idea which had had its day? Or was the very notion of liberation theology one which could no longer be sustained - was it dead, or at least moribund, as Cardinal Ratsinger had recently proclaimed? Was it the universal ascendancy of the neo-liberal model and in Britain, the failure of the newly elected Labour government to significantly challenge it? Or a sense of the post-modernist despair in the absence of alternative socio-economic models which prompted people to seek out niches in the structures, in which they could cultivate their own little gardens until such time as a new "grand narrative" once more became the order of the day? Earlier Consultations had offered space for the exploration and sharing of a number of disparate agendas – a feature which had made previous Consultations sometimes a site of conflict. How far had their adherents now established autonomous areas of activity in which allies had already been identified and programmes of action pursued? How far was it that some of the agendas previously promoted had been absorbed, superficially at least, into the structural thinking of the major churches, making this convocation of dissidents less necessary?

On a more practical level, was it that with voluntary organisations being increasingly strapped for cash, even the relatively modest expense could not be justified for some sponsored in the past, or that the demands on professionals' time now left no space for a weekend of reflection?

These thoughts, of course are to some degree the fruit of reflection after the weekend was over. In the immediacy of the event, more urgent organisational decisions take precedence. In terms of methodology, the process which had been adopted for the 1995 weekend was repeated and led to the formation of three discussion groups: one concentrating on strategies for tackling forms of exclusion, another on ways of confronting or negotiating with conservative or traditional structures, and a third on approaches to the Millennium. Plenary inputs included a report on the Fourth General Assembly of the Ecumenical Association of Third World Theologians by Bridget Rees, an account of a visit paid by Ian Fraser to members of the erstwhile "underground" church in the former Czechoslovakia, and a resume of a social survey into *What Women Want* by Myra Poole. During the story group sessions, Projects, Issues and Faith Journeys, Inderjit Bhogal spoke on the Methodist report *The Cities*; David Peel on the Cedarwood community on the Meadow Well estate, North Shields; Geraldine Poole on a controversial Black-run College in Liverpool; Moby Farrands explored the dichotomy between maintaining church structures and building community; Janet Hodgson spoke of the faith journey involved in moving from a privileged white background in South Africa through radical political and theological dissent to challenging the assumptions of white privileged people in Britain – "from black theology to duvet theology"; and David Maggs told the story of his own journey – Changes, Ideals, Compromises – working for justice in diverse ways in a variety of European contexts. Frank Regan, a Columban Father with over twenty years' experience of working with workers' organisations and grass roots communities in Peru, gave the final reflection.

In contrast to some previous Consultations, there was only a minimum of conflict involved. The ambience was one of tolerance. In the deliberations there was a more marked disposition to listen to others and less tendency to parade the banner of one's own particular theology of liberation. Was it in fact too bland, almost "cosy"? Too lacking in creative dialectic? Most people, nevertheless, appeared to have found the weekend of value and expressed a desire to keep in touch in some way during the long intervals between Consultations.

The idea of an informal newsletter, touched upon on previous occasions, was raised again, and we agreed to explore the possibility of this not only for those present, but for other interested parties. Such a project seems viable and was realised later in 1999. In his final reflection, Frank Regan quoted Pablo Richard:

> "*We live in the time of ants and spiders. The elephants have already moved through.*"

It is the nature of spiders to weave webs, and this has been for many years a significant symbol for Las Casas. Such a newsletter, perhaps, can provide further strands for the web.

And we fixed the 6th Consultation and Celebration – 1st-3rd October, 1999, at Wistaston.

---

[1] One affinity group, on Poverty and Deprivation, is described by John Vincent in "Liberation Theology in Britain", **Liberation Theology UK** (UTU 1995) pp 15-37, pp 34-35.

[2] Pablo Richard, in an interview for the magazine "Utopias" (No. 37, August 1996), "La Iglesia Catolica Hay una Ausencia de Biblia Tremenda".

[3] See Margaret Walsh, "Still Hoping", in **Gospel from the City**, (UTU, 1997), pp 64-75.

# John Vincent

# A NEW THEOLOGY AND SPIRITUALITY

The development of a British Liberation Theology is carried on at different levels. The Boff brothers say that liberation theology is done at three levels – the professional (academic), the pastoral, and the popular.[1] Mainly, theological publications operate at the academic and pastoral levels. The writings in this British Liberation Theology series operate mainly at the pastoral and popular levels, though mostly through practitioner-theologians who themselves are aware of the academic level, but especially speak on the basis of engagement, if not physical existence, among the deprived in one form or another.

This volume and the previous one, *Gospel from the City*, are mostly pieces written by practitioners, but even more by practitioners who are reflective practitioner-theologians, who use the Gospel as a means of discernment and empowerment. They are often also theological teachers. Moreover the Gospel might well have been a decisive element in the "call" which led them to be where they are.

This piece attempts to pull together some elements of a British Liberation Theology and Spirituality, in the light of the contributions so far. What are the lines and characteristics of the Spirituality visible or hidden here?

---

**John Vincent is part-time Lecturer and MPhil/PhD Supervisor at UTU. His forthcoming book, Hope from the City, (Epworth Press, 2000) continues the story of inner city Sheffield and the ecumenical mission.**

What are the dominant and special tones and emphases implied or explicit in the realm of Theology?

I am not concerned here with the implications for Theology as a whole of the new Theology described here. On this, the comments of Chris Rowland (GC, pp. 126-131) remain important – and await response!

I discern seven significant features, as evidenced by our three volumes, *Liberation Theology UK* (LTh), *Gospel from the City* (GC) and *Liberation Spirituality* (LS).

**1. God's Realm as Presence.**

There is a clear sense that the Kingdom of God is happening, that the Kingdom of God realities are taking place. It is not at all the old "liberal" idea that by our social or community or even personal work, we are "building the Kingdom of God". Neither is it that contemporary political movements can be identified with the Kingdom, as Andrew Bradstock makes clear (LTh, pp. 100-103). Rather it is that the Kingdom of God suddenly becomes present, suddenly becomes a reality, in happenings, events, people, relationships, movements, projects and communities.

Thus Margaret Walsh reflects that she had to rediscover how "to wait and sit around with nothing to do". She goes on

> "Now, I happily wander around the balconies, 'loitering with intent', and looking for God and the signs of the Kingdom in unexpected places and people. God definitely has a sense of humour!" (GC, p. 72)

The implication is that the Kingdom of God is already present, and that any ministry is at least in part a ministry relating to an already existing reality at work among the people, and to a God already working among them. This makes one of Duncan Wilson's Gospel "values" – "That those not within the Church are not necessarily far from the Kingdom of God." (GC, p. 104)

Alan Powers now (LS, pp. 30-41) names a few "moments" from the preceding volume, which he sees as indicating events when "the Angel appears", "the Eagle strikes", "the Dead God resurrects" or "the Galilean walks". A spirituality results which is a spirituality of being prepared to be surprised, overtaken, overcome by the unexpected revelations of God. God's "sovereign realm" is above all where God's "sovereign freedom" chooses that it will be, and that is in the places of human need, as was the case in Jesus' life and work.

Hence, Christine Dodd seeks to "liberate spirituality (LS, pp. 19-22), so that it becomes an "incarnational spirituality" (p.20) which "allows us to engage in the 'liberation project' which God has for all" (p.22).

> "Contemplation gives us the 'squint' with which we glimpse those Kingdom moments and events where God is already acting, and to begin to co-operate with God in that action." (p.20)

The "grandeur of God" is thus in the inner city, the poor, the abused, or the bereaved, "in these people who 'incarnate' God in those situations" (p.23). God's Realm is especially present among the "Underclass", says Laurie Green (GC., p. 124) or the urban poor (Vincent, pp. 106-7), who are those who empathise with Gospel people, and celebrate the same Kingdom realities.

God's Realm is present in small, sudden, unrepeatable, radical occasions when people, communities and situations become parts of "life structured God's way", in Ian Fraser's phrase (LS, p.42). But that also means "setting up signs of the Kingdom", and at times "confrontation of the present order in order to turn it into God's order" (ibid). And that means politics.

## 2. God's Realm as Politics.

Ian Fraser describes how this works out in relation to a specific political issue, and names elements in "the gift of Discernment" – Research, Prayer, Selection, Timing, Alongsidedness (LS, p. 44).

The political action of disciples today inevitably "confronts the powers", as Laurie Green points out (GC, pp. 121-124). Yet the lines of such action take their cue from Jesus' presence and practice, as Inderjit Bhogal describes:

> Jesus cared deeply for the state of the nation, and demonstrated this by:
> Breaking down the Boundaries;
> Proclaiming that God's love is not restricted by boundaries, and comes close to people;
> Including those who have been excluded;

Eating with anyone who would eat with him. (LS, p.49)

Precisely this, says Inderjit, is needed now in "our contemporary world of ethnic cleansing" and inter-racial strife (LS, p.51).

The political area of the Kingdom activity, in these pieces, reflects the same ethos as do the small presences. The political activity seeks to reflect the dynamics of the Kingdom's presence within specific areas of public life, but it does not fundamentally alter the character or style of those dynamics. It is, as Inderjit says, political holiness. Either way, the world has to make the best of it. It suffices that the Kingdom has become present (cf. Lk. 10.11).

The actual political activities described by Ian Fraser and Inderjit Bhogal come mainly under the headings of "unilateral initiative" – a group or individual pioneering some new policy or attitude – or else symbolic action – a public protest to draw attention to some evil or injustice. Some of the frustrations at the Consultations and Celebrations, described by Mike Simpson and Joan Sharples (LS, pp. 74-94), were due to people expecting that the political scene, being the arena and background for our work (cf. p. 87), as such could become the field for Liberation Theology practice. However, Andrew Bradstock's account of Nicaragua reveals that community is a more possible field (LTh, pp. 99-103). And the Jubilee 2000 campaign (Bridget Rees, LS, pp. 10-14) will doubtless not win the political fulfilment we optimistically hoped for.

Inderjit Bhogal implies that perhaps we are pointers and prophets, first, rather than politicians – and such "political holiness" (SL, pp. 46, 59) is, not only desperately needed, but also our most appropriate way of acting. Anger and mercy are our way, based on divine anger and mercy (pp. 55-57), and they have specific political implications for Christians (p.58).

Politicians writing legislation might occasionally be of our number. But we have also to keep our powder dry for the next foray, and make sure that our demands for justice, on the basis of humanity and of theology (cf. p. 58) are not modified or tempered by the political exigencies of the moment, however much they are properly related to them and thrown up by them.

**3. Receiving God's Realm as a Child.**

This "down-sizing" of expectations regarding political hopes corresponds to a general emphasis in our writings upon the grass-roots, human, street-level, and "bottom-up" character of Jesus' work and teaching. What Inderjit calls for is "political saints", who are "the ones who identify with the poorest and most vulnerable, and who take risks of faith" (LS, p.59). I comment on the people and communities at the bottom of society today who identify with and see their own work as continuing Jesus's (Vincent, GC, pp. 105-113). Their life "free of race and class and economic and cultural distinction" puts them alongside Jesus and his disciples (GC, p.112).

Characteristic of this emphasis on the small is that the words of perception, or significance, of mercy or of judgement come from children. Thus Jane Grinonneau tells of how the child can be "an Agent of the Kingdom" to the Church. The key story is retold by Alan Powers (LS, pp. 33-34), in which Jane Grinonneau concludes: "In so many ways, the children showed us how to be open, powerless and free in the truth of Christ" (GC p.28).

And Jan Royan tells the story of burying a favourite cat, and being helped by Jenny, a 12-year old from the council estate beside Chapel House. Jan found herself crying, and Jenny said "Don't cry, Jan. Topsy's happy now". They put stones on to the grave to prevent dogs from digging it up, and Jenny says: "Shouldn't we say a prayer for Topsy, Jan?" (GC, p.44).

Of course, it is not straightforward. Duncan Wilson reflects on the youngsters, "more bored than bad, who needed to show they could leave an impression" by gratuitous vandalism, who stole the old ladies' handbags though they ministered to them, and stole from the jumble sale held for their club.

> Small hands stuff selected items up oversized jackets – this is after all the enterprise culture and they have learned already that only number one is going to look after number one. That is, unless by some miracle they become puzzled by their acceptance among those they have already wronged. (GC, p. 94)

Duncan says it is about "the cost of including everyone within the circle of Christ's friendship".

Jane Grinonneau raises the question about Jesus' use of children as a model for the church. What would happen if a whole church were to be built on the model of the child? These questions are raised, but also in part answered, in the stories of the Christian communities at Shiregreen and Wincobank which I tell in *Hope from the City.*[2] Perhaps it is easier for congregations which are themselves often wounded people, to manifest the simple, straightforward, human-shaped, vulnerable and totally flexible character of a Church in the image of the child. An organisational structure emerges which is ad hoc, tentative, unpredictable and based on easy and immediate communication – like the Grimesthorpe congregation described here by Grace Vincent (LS, pp. 68-73). A childlike Church!

Childlike perhaps, but a theology of the Church as the Body of Christ seems much more coherent with such congregational life than with that of the larger, more organised, more balanced, perhaps more middle class church. Vulnerability, argues Christine Dodd (LS, pp. 25-26) must be at the heart of everything, as it is at the heart of God and the whole ecological system. Jan Royan says (LS, P.65)

> "Jesus trusted people, and it made him vulnerable. But this was his choice. Better to be vulnerable and to be betrayed, than always to see people as your enemy, constantly to mistrust their motives."

God's Realm is received in vulnerability as we receive a child who is vulnerable.

## 4. Evangelisation by the Poor.

There is a strong element of being evangelised by the poor and the marginalised in the urban areas. The practitioner theologian does not "bring" the Gospel, but is rather brought into the Gospel, or aspects of it, through the experiences of the poor, and the experiences of working with them. Margaret Walsh thus writes that "it is such a privilege to find this same Jesus among the poor in Wolverhampton."

> To be honest, I often feel that I have only begun to understand the Jesus of the gospels in the last few years. It is certainly the most formative experience I have had. Living among the poor, I can see and hear those who followed Jesus in a very real way as I contemplate these Gospel scenes. Jesus did not associate with the poor because of their virtue, but because of their suffering and their powerlessness and also because of their simple, childlike faith and trust. I am always struck by their humility and also by their desperation when they come forward in public to lay their wretchedness and sin at his feet. I suppose too that those who have so little in terms of status and material

> possessions are more free to reach out and experience the riches of Christ. (GC, p.66)

The Gospel which is thus disclosed is also a quite specific understanding of the Gospel. The good news of Jesus emerges as part of a process whereby the individual comes into a new orientation and understanding, which basically affirms and supports their own existing lifestyle and commitments. "Conversion" or "contextualisation" does not take a person out of their life commitments and lifestyle. Thus Diane Butler writes about how her "call" is to remain with unemployed working class people on a deprived housing estate where "help has arisen out of friendship rather than power and dominance."

> Life shouts at me that liberation will never be tied up with becoming affluent. It is about recognising our interdependence rather than our independence, struggling to work out our humanity in mutuality, and having a sense of belonging. This is "what it is to be human". And I want to stake my life on these things not because Jesus tells me, though it may be the case they turn out to be what he taught and was about. It is more that I found and owned them for myself through my life experience. It is for me the right way to be in the world. (GC, p.36)

Diane Butler thinks that "the life I am living is the life that Jesus was talking about". She does not have to "change" to become a disciple on the Jesus model. Jesus also chose to live among the poor (p.37).

Again, Jan Royan speaks of the "Mutuality of Evangelism", and the way that the people with learning difficulties "like God, show me unconditional love", and "show me the way to be human" (LS, pp. 62-63), or how daily starting again with repeatedly offending youngsters is only "what we ask of God when we pray for forgiveness" (LS, p.65).

Thus Laurie Green sees "the Underclass", in Jesus' day and in ours today, as the crucial, dynamic community, the "sinners and social outcasts", the ochlos, which participates in the incoming Kingdom (GC, pp. 117-125). And I argue that "There is a new hearing of the Gospel on our streets as the story of Jesus in his time strikes home in the lives of urban people today" (GC, p.114), so that "disciples at the bottom of British society begin very tentatively to feel that the Gospel could possibly even be on their side" (GC, p.115).

Thus, the Christian in the wider church today is faced by a concrete embodiment of at least some aspects of Christian discipleship in the person of the poor. The poverty of Christ in the poverty of the poor person calls to the would-be disciple. Here is already an *imitatio Christi*, which preaches the Gospel to the Christian everywhere. It remains to be seen how far our mainly middle class Church can take it on board. Luke's Gospel, says Chris Rowland, is a model for middle-class cultured disciples who still want to hold to the radicality of Jesus' Gospel to the Poor (LTh, pp. 41-54). Somehow or other, the whole church must learn from our own "Oppressed People as Mediators of God", in Chris's words (GC, p.130).

## 5. Secular Jesus Spirituality

What all this means is perhaps that the beginnings of a post-Christian, secular, grass-roots spirituality are beginning to appear, based on what Moby Farrands calls "the way in which in very small ways the Gospels are being acted out today" (GC, p.63), through people acting like those in the Jesus stories (GC, p. 58).

Perhaps we are discovering that Christian spirituality is distinctive only when it is Jesus-praxis-centred. Genuine spirituality comes from the guts of the Christ-shaped revelation in the midst of the human, from the mystery of the Corpus Christi, the Body of Christ, incarnating itself at the depths of existence, where the lineaments of humanity, salvation, redemption and holiness are manifest, consumed and lived off, in the midst of the hostility, sightlessness and unconverted minds of incredulous believers and sceptics. The thirty years since Vatican II and the beginnings of theologies of liberation have witnessed the relocation of spirituality in the imitation of the deeds of Christ, in the practice of the Kingdom of God, in the lifestyle of Jesus, and in the solidarity of disciples in struggles for justice and peace. And some are now living by these things, as Duncan Wilson observes from Inner City Churches (GC, pp. 86-104).

This Spirituality of Jesus-centred Liberation and Wholeness is well expressed by Casadaliga and Vigil. They describe first the spirituality of all human beings as such, which "drinks from sources of life: history, social conditions, praxis, reflection, wisdom, contemplation – all that feeds the heart and mind."[3] They then describe the explicitly Christian elements which go to make up "The Liberating Spirit of Jesus Christ". Here, the decisive elements are the Historical Jesus, the distinctively Christian God, the Trinity, "Reign-Focus", Incarnation, and Following Jesus. These in turn create highly distinctive versions of "Contemplatives in Liberation", Prayer Life, and

Prophecy, and become visible in "Putting Love into Practice", in the Option for the Poor, and in Cross/Conflict/Martyrdom.

Thus, Christian Liberation Spirituality has a focus on Jesus and a focus on secular reality. These both "open it up" and "tie it down", both open it out to universal significance, and tie it down to specific significance.

> Because it is a "Christian" spirituality of liberation, the spirituality of liberation seeks to be a spirituality based on Jesus' own spirit (or Spirit – the ipsissima intentio Iesu). It tries to make its primary focus following Jesus and continuing the struggle he waged. It does not give importance to side issues in the Christian universe.
>
> At the same time, as a spirituality "of liberation", it concentrates on what is most universal, urgent and decisive in the human universe: the situation of the poor and their plea for life, for justice, for peace, for freedom, against domination and oppression. No one who does not hear and absorb this central demand of the real world can understand the spirituality of liberation or make it coherent and credible.[4]

It is surely this fundamental humanity-centredness and Christ-centredness together which feeds the incredible variety of people with perceptibly alternative theologies and practices, evident in the Consultations and Celebrations of which Mike Simpson and Joan Sharples write (LS, pp. 74-94). Indeed, the occasionally violent or difficult expressions of their commitments indicates how each Liberation Theology practitioner embodies within her/himself a unique and special protest at some particular domination or oppression, provoking their own Christ-centred discipleship praxis.

**6. Secularity and EnChristedness.**

Our Theology and our Spirituality are thus characterised by total secularity and total en-Christedness.

The total secularity is clear. We are only being human. We are only doing what any human being can do. So Frank Regan writes of the 70,000 people in Birmingham for the 1998 Jubilee demonstration:

> In Birmingham on May 16th, for two minutes the throng of 70,000 made noise, whistled and shouted for new life for one

> billion people. Could that have been the new song, the pentecostal hymn praising the God who calls from out of the chaos of our present situation, "Come follow me?"[5]

Thus, activities of contemporary people, believers and non-believers, and mainly in this case the non-poor, become part of liberation practice.

Similarly, Alan Powers describes secular happenings which are significant and moving, and identifies them as manifestations of God's unexpected sovereign freedom "for us", as and when God chooses, but also in decisive ways determined by the dominical commandment to see God in the neighbour and to meet Christ in the concrete person who represents Christ and the issues of Christ for us. The Christian is pivotal not because of any religiosity but because "I have been given eyes to see the signs of God's Kingdom in some of the events around me" (LS, p39)

Indeed, the absence of the "signs of God's Kingdom" have to be sensed. Liberation and wholeness are needed in the midst of oppressive structures, non-fulfilling pretensions, and violence against humanity. As Inderjit Bhogal observes:

> God wants all people to have life in all its fullness. The vision of God is portrayed in Scripture as everyone having a home, with a garden, and with a tree in the garden. This is the Biblical image of Shalom. It is God's will that people should have the freedom and resources to "build houses and live in them, plant vines and eat their fruit" (Isa. 65.21). For this to be achieved, everything that prevents it should be brought to an end, such as poverty, debts, enslavement, exploitation of land. (LS, p56)

Thus, whatever the contemporary issues of the "secular world", whether described as "post modern" or not, the issues of ultimacy, of Kingdom, of en-Christedness, are present. Precisely being prophetic and faithful in the midst of this is what Inderjit describes as the "Holiness" we need. Wherever secularity is felt at its most vicious, the Christ disciples are present, in equal secularity, "following their incarnate God" (a phrase of Isaac Watts).

## 7. "Spiritual Exercises"

Spirituality, we conclude, is about how we become and support ourselves as people within the Christ-mysteries on earth. Spirituality is following the Jesus of the streets, feeling, acting, loving and being as the Gospel Jesus did.

Beyond that, Spirituality is the "wells" deep within each of us which sustain this discernment and this discipleship. It is about the deeps within our own personalities which minister and recreate discernment and discipleship.

Christine Dodd describes how Spirituality in more traditional guises, needs to be "liberated" in order to function in these ways. The "Spiritual Exercises" of Ignatius of Loyola and the classic tradition need to be seen today as being ways of "being liberated" from conventional religion – into God, into ourselves, into discipleship, into the world. Our "spiritual exercises" must support the incarnate God people –

> "Those who give themselves away in myriads of diverse ways, those who unite others in their brokenness, who exercise their variety of gifts in the pain"
>
> "A new exodus is under way for individuals, for communities, for those who are still enslaved." (p.23)

The revival of Spirituality in our time has so far been about the riches of spirituality within many traditions being rediscovered by contemporary Christians. Clearly, many people have been helped by all this. And the aim of such "exercises" has always been discernment and discipleship. And perhaps there are no short cuts. But the evidence of Jan Royan here is surely salutary. She describes "an underground river, which is the source of true life" for her.

> "This river of life is in every created being, and owes its existence to God, the Creator of all life. Tapping into this river in myself and discovering it in others is the source of my spirituality for the inner city." (LS, p.61)

She then goes on to describe "some of the people, events, stories and thoughts that have helped resource my spirituality."

What Jan describes is, in fact, a set of "conclusions" from her experience, which become guidelines for her journey – a set of very down-to-earth "rules" or "mottos" which constitute contemporary "spiritual exercises" for disciples following the model of incarnation and prophetic living (LS, pp. 61-67).

Jan's exercises are the kind of truths often expressed in inner city fellowships, in my experience. How all these manifest themselves in specific prayer, devotion and worship now becomes an issue for us all. The

Grimesthorpe Methodists certainly are working on a non-Catholic devotional tradition. But their worship, as described by Grace Vincent, has some of the same ethos of a deeper catholic, universal, gut-based spirituality, properly and refreshingly at odds with this year's incredibly insensitive and dully "orthodox" *Methodist Worship Book*[6]. On reflection, the *Worship Book* seems a striking instance of spirituality as domestication rather than liberation, as Bridget Rees would say (LS, p.15).

The God being worshipped or discerned or served in the many Grimesthorpes of the contemporary church is the God of the streets, where, as Grace Vincent says, "the context is tiny, but the brief is vast" (LS, p.73). That sounds like a motto for the new Theology and Spirituality "from the bottom", "following the incarnate God"! Perhaps, eventually, there will be some "fruits" to set beside those of traditional spiritualities!

Meantime, we stay with the incarnation and with people of incarnation – where, often as not, the Lord's people are also prophets!

---

[1] Leonardo Boff & Clodovis Boff, **Introducing Liberation Theology**, Burns & Oates, 1987, pp. 11-14
[2] John Vincent, **Hope from the City**, Epworth Press, 2000
[3] Pedro Casaldaliga and Jose Maria Vigil, **The Spirituality of Liberation**, Burns & Oates, 1994, p. 14
[4] Casaldaliga and Vigil, p. 204
[5] Frank Regan SSC, "Mission: Will There be Faith …" in **British Liberation Theology Newsletter**, No. 1, February 1999, p.5
[6] **A Methodist Worship Book**, Methodist Publishing House, 1999

# LETTERS

## RESPONSE TO GOSPEL FROM THE CITY

Dear Editors,
Thank yoü for *Gospel from the City.* May I congratulate you on this stimulating series of publications. But I would like to make a suggestion. There seems to be a need for more dialogue among the contributors. The parallels drawn by Jan Royan between people living in the Flower Estate, Sheffield, and the people of the La Pita Co-operative, Nicaragua, are fascinating and important. The differences are significant but the similarities cannot be ignored, e.g. in relation to violence and drunkenness, and the spending of money on festive occasions.

In the letter from Lyn Atterbury the point is rightly made that "both the poor and the rich are locked into the consumerist treadmill". And this is increasingly becoming true not only of the developed world, but also wherever the global economy pushes its media and advertising tentacles into local cultures.

I missed in the latter section of the book adequate theological wrestling with the implications of this change in the world scene. I felt that we were being encouraged to think too simplistically and statically about the "Underclass" as the "only" (Laurie Green, p.124) group in society open to the challenge and hope of Liberation Theology. I know there is still a great deal of truth in this approach, but I would plead for more reflection on the complex issues created by the glimpses of the consumerist society now being given to the poorest of the world. Is this beginning to create a new materialist outlook on life which must change the more hopeful picture of the "Underclass" which Liberation Theology has so far been able to work with?

Yours sincerely,

Rt Rev Tony Dumper
Wolverhampton

Laurie Green in, "The Jesus of the Inner City" in *Urban Christ: Responses to John Vincent*, ed. Ian K Duffield, Urban Theology Unit 1997, pp. 24-33, argues that "those who have made it" also need liberation (pp. 30-33). Editor.

# CHRONICLE

## THE INSTITUTE FOR BRITISH LIBERATION THEOLOGY

The annual Institute for British Liberation Theology met at the UTU in Sheffield for three days Tuesday-Thursday, 22-24 July 1997 with the main theme "Gospel from the City", and 21-23 July 1998 with the main theme "Liberation Spirituality". The 1999 Consultation meets 20-22 July with the main theme "Bible and Practice", which is also the theme of the next BLT volume, due for publication in 2001. The Institute is open to everyone interested. Participants contribute a small charge, and arrange their own accommodation or pay for rooms at UTU. Please write with offers of contributions for the next Institutes, which will be Tuesday-Thursday, 11-13 July 2000, on the theme "Black Theology" and Tuesday-Thursday, 17-19 July 2001. Enquiries to the Joint Co-ordinators: Rev Dr John Vincent, 178 Abbeyfield Road, Sheffield S4 7AY or: Ms Bridget Rees, 440 Huddersfield Road, Mirfield, WF14 0EE

## THE BRITISH LIBERATION THEOLOGY CONSULTATION AND CELEBRATION

The British Liberation Theology Consultation and Celebration is a bi-annual event held at Wistaston Hall, near Crewe. It is a sharing and supportive fellowship for people working in liberation theology style projects and ministries. The sixth Consultation and Celebration will take place on Friday-Sunday, 1-3 October 1999, then in October 2001. Joint Co-ordinators are: Mr Mike Simpson and Mrs Joan Sharples, c/o 16 Wellington Road, Nantwich CW5 7BH

## BRITISH LIBERATION THEOLOGY NEWSLETTER

We welcome the arrival of the Newsletter, which is designed as an informal communication between practitioners and others interested. The first issue was published in February 1999, and six-monthly issues are envisaged. Details from: Mr Mike Simpson and Mrs Joan Sharples, c/o 16 Wellington Road, Nantwich CW5 7BH

## THE FORUM FOR BRITISH BLACK THEOLOGY

The Institute for British Black Theology is an annual meeting of workers and writers of British Black and Asian Theologies. Contributions are invited, which may become part of a proposed Journal. The Institute takes place at UTU in Sheffield. Future dates are Saturday 10 July 1999 and in July of subsequent years. Enquiries to the Chair: Rev Inderjit Bhogal, 210 Abbeyfield Road, Sheffield S4 7AZ

## DOCTORAL PROGRAMME IN CONTEXTUAL, URBAN AND LIBERATION THEOLOGIES

A MPhil/PhD course in Contextual, Urban and Liberation Theologies, with Dr John Vincent as Supervisor, and an Associate Supervisor from the Biblical Studies Department of Sheffield University, uses the Urban Theology Unit as base. Degrees are awarded by Sheffield University. Groups of candidates meet quarterly at UTU for 3-day periods over the first two years, of the part-time course, then single days. Enquiries to: Dr John Vincent, Urban Theology Unit, 210 Abbeyfield Road, Sheffield S4 7AZ.

## LAS CASAS NETWORK

This network takes its name from Bartholome de las Casas, a Dominican priest who in the sixteenth century devoted his life to struggling against the brutality and exploitation of the Spanish Conquest of the Americas.

The core of the network is a small ecumenical base community with contacts throughout the country, and a number abroad. Its initial aim is to focus attention on Latin America and to provide information in English from a variety of sources, in order to expand knowledge of the area, to promote an awareness of its problems, and to suggest courses of action open to those who are concerned about them. A major part of the work in this context is currently concerned with Colombia, Las Casas being responsible for the co-ordination of the Colombia Forum human-rights network.

Secondly, and of major importance in its present praxis, is the furtherance of an understanding of Third World liberation theologies and the promotion of appropriate contextual theologies in Britain. Las Casas is responsible for the convening and organisation of the British Liberation Theology Consultation and Celebration which takes place every two years.

Its resources centre in Nantwich has a wide range of books on development, human rights and environmental issues, on liberation, peace and creation theologies, and missiology, reverse mission and inter-faith dialogue. Office and Resource Centre: 16 Wellington Road, Nantwich, Cheshire, CW5 7BH.

## URBAN THEOLOGY PROGRAMME

John Vincent will act as Consultant and Tutor for a 2-month Urban Theology Programme at St Deiniol's Library in October-November 1999. There will be Urban Theology Workshops throughout October, with an Open Series of Saturday Consultations. Urban Church members, workers and ministers are invited to apply for Bursaries and Scholarships. Details from: Rev Peter Francis, St Deiniol's Library, Hawarden, Flintshire CH5 3DF

## RADICAL VOICES ON THE BIBLE

This is a writing and research project to provide a companion and guide to interpretations of biblical texts which are biased towards social analysis and a radical, liberationist perspective. It is designed for practitioners in ministry, students and academics interested in either liberation theology, urban theology, or feminist theology and practical action. It will be a source of reference which cannot be found elsewhere. The first volume will focus on Jesus and the synoptic gospels. Other volumes will cover the whole of the Bible: Johannine Books; Paul's Letters; Acts and Other NT Writings; Torah; Kingdoms; Prophets; Wisdom. Contact: Revd Dr Ian K Duffield and Revd Dr Robin Pagan, Urban Theology Unit, 210 Abbeyfield Road, Sheffield S4 7AZ

## REMEMBERING THE DIGGERS

While the Levellers, Tolpuddle Martyrs and other heroes of our radical history are remembered each year on appropriate dates, the 17th-century communist group know as the Diggers have generally been forgotten. But not any longer! This April, 350 years to the month after they set up their commune on St George's Hill near Weybridge in Surrey, their courage, vision and heroism were celebrated in and around the area where they operated. Thanks to the efforts of a loosely-knit group of enthusiasts and landrights activists known as 'Diggers 350', a series of events was held in the Weybridge and Walton area, including a public meeting on 1st April (the exact date the Diggers began occupying St George's Hill); a march up to the

Hill (now one of the plushest and most exclusive residential areas in the country!); an exhibition in the Elmbridge Museum; and a conference at St Mary's Church, Walton, where the Diggers were imprisoned in 1649.

All events attracted a good deal of support and interest: around 2000 people visited the exhibition, 300 joined the march and pageant up to St George's Hill, the national and local media ran stories and features, and activists, politicians, artists and academics like Michael Foot, Leon Rosselson, George Monbiot, Alistair MacIntosh, Ian Saunders, Ann Hughes, Elaine Hobby and Gerald Aylmer participated in the various events. Sculptor Andrew Whittle produced a beautiful memorial stone featuring the words which inspired the Digger leader Gerrard Winstanley to begin his project – 'Worke Together, Eat Bread Together' – though permission for a permanent site on the Hill is still being negotiated. Partly to draw attention to this, and to how little things have changed since the Diggers' day, an occupation of some land on the Hill was staged to follow the march. This ended following a hearing in the High Court a week or so later.

Having at last put the Diggers back on the radical calendar, it is hoped that a suitable memorial to them will be held in April every year. Better late than never!

ANDREW BRADSTOCK

## WEST YORKSHIRE LIBERATION THEOLOGY GROUP

There are over 30 people in the West Yorkshire area who have shown interest in Liberation Theology through the Faith in Community Project – an exciting new venture set up by the Community of the Resurrection with the Churches in West Yorkshire in 1997 as part of the Mirfield Centre, with Bridget Rees as Director. Part of the original vision for the Faith in Community Project was that it might help people in West Yorkshire to reflect on their faith and how it impacted on their life and that of the people around them, especially work on what a Liberation Theology for West Yorkshire might look like. One group is now meeting in the Leeds area every two months. The group works by mutual sharing, learning from each other's ministries, and meeting at each other's places of life and work. Before the departure of the Director of the Centre and Project, it had been envisaged that other groups might meet in similar ways to the Leeds group. Details from: Liberation Theology Group, The Faith in Community Project, The Mirfield Centre, Stocksbank Road, Mirfield, WF14 0BW; Or: Roger Harrington, 227 Beech Lane, Leeds 9